Comments About

When the Other Guy's Price Is Lower

by James M. Bleech and Dr. David G. Mutchler

"*When the Other Guy's Price Is Lower* is essential reading for anyone who sells anything, whether novice or veteran. Bleech and Mutchler do a superior job of explaining how selling has changed, why common methods don't work and what to do about it."

Paula Ancona
Scripps Howard News Service
Business Columnist and Author

"This book is a winner—destined to lead the sales profession into the 21st century! Bleech and Mutchler offer a revolutionary and inspiring message, showing salespeople how to outsell the competition—even when the other guy's price is lower!"

Og Mandino
Best Selling Author and Speaker

"At last, a book that teaches salespeople how to be different in today's market where competing products, prices, and services are becoming more alike every day!"

Money Lines Magazine

"Destined to become *the* sales book for every serious salesperson and sales manager. Quite simply, there isn't another approach that comes close!"

J. Thomas Solano
CEO
Information Systems, Inc.

"Usually when I hear of a good book on sales, I pick up a copy, read the first two or three chapters, and then pass it on to our VP of Sales for his review. This is the first time I have ever felt compelled to read a sales book from cover to cover. And by the way, when I handed this one over to my VP of Sales, I didn't say, 'See what you think.' Instead I said, 'Do it now!' "

Anthony W. Brown
CEO
Yoxall Electric Supply, Inc.

"*When the Other Guy's Price Is Lower* presents new and practical sales strategies in an organized and tangible format—a must-read for any sales professional!"

Elizabeth Pagano
Nashville Banner
Business Reporter

"While others may be looking for a magical approach to selling, we've found it. Our question will never be whether or not to use an approach other than Leadership Selling, but rather, how can we best master this system in the shortest possible period of time?"

Cork Motsett
VP of Sales
Shred All, Inc.

"Bleech and Mutchler have done it again by hitting the bulls-eye on the central sales issue facing corporate America today—price! Every sales manager and every salesperson who reads this book will be better prepared to outsell the competition, regardless of price."

Roy Mohrman
President
Handling Systems Engineering, Inc.

"By insisting that everyone of our salespeople use Leadership Selling, our total sales output has tripled in one short year, and our products are never the lowest priced. What can I say except, while other selling approaches claim to be the best, this one truly works!"

Chuck Parliment
Vice President
Zambetti Steel

When The Other Guy's Price Is Lower

You Can Still Make The Sale

Introducing the LEADERSHIP SELLING SYSTEM

When The Other Guy's Price Is Lower
You Can Still Make The Sale

Introducing the LEADERSHIP SELLING SYSTEM

James M. Bleech and Dr. David G. Mutchler

LIFETIME BOOKS

2131 Hollywood Blvd., Suite 305
Hollywood, FL 33020

WHEN THE OTHER GUY'S PRICE IS LOWER

Manufactured in the United States of America
1 2 3 4 5 6 7 8 9 0

Library of Congress Cataloging-in-Publication Data

Bleech, James M., 1948-
        When the other guy's price is lower : you can still make the sale
        / James M. Bleech, David G. Mutchler.
                p. cm.
        ISBN 0-8119-0811-9
        1. Selling. 2. Selling—Psychological aspects. I. Mutchler,
David G., 1942-   . II. Title.
        HF5438.25.B565   1996
        658.85—dc20   95-44700
                                                                CIP

Acknowledgments

Where do we begin to thank all of the people who have been a positive influence on writing this book? Special thanks go to:

• First and foremost, the many thousands of salespeople, their managers, and their vice presidents of sales with whom we've worked, and from whom we've learned untold lessons and valuable applications of Leadership Selling.

• The late David Sandler for his sales mentorship.

• The many, many sales trainers with whom we are familiar who have given pointers on both how, and how not, to sell in the fast-paced economy in which we now live.

• Carol Waite and Gwyn Bersie for their tireless and outstanding editorial help.

• Our families for their patience, understanding, and unwavering support.

Dedication

For every salesperson in the world who is
seeking a selling approach that is both effective
and professional—one that *finally* allows him to
hold his head up high and proudly proclaim,

"I am a salesperson!"

Contents

Contents

Foreword

As a matter of record, my career spans a quarter of a century as an accomplished sales professional and successful executive. Over those twenty-five years, I have seen different selling approaches and techniques come and go—from product demonstration, to feature and benefit selling, to convince-selling techniques using strong closing skills, to need-assessment selling. Each approach was effective in its own way and in its own time. The problem now, however, is that they are all old and outdated, and therefore not up to the challenges facing us in the business world today.

When I first read *When the Other Guy's Price Is Lower* (thereby being introduced to the concept of Leadership Selling), I was pleased to find a selling approach that is new and refreshing—one that is suited to the space-age economy in which we now live.

Like most businesses, technology is changing our approach to business as never before. As a CEO of a company approaching a billion dollars in annual revenues, I am not the least bit shy to admit that I have needs for this remarkably new approach to selling. Furthermore, I have total confidence that it will help me continue to grow and my company to prosper in light of the rapid change that we are faced with daily.

Leadership Selling is a sales approach that offers a nontraditional yet highly effective system for problem solving—one that will clearly give you a strategic advantage over your competition. It is an approach that challenges you and causes you to stretch, and as a result, to excel at the profession of selling.

I say to you without hesitation that, in my experience, Leadership Selling is the most advanced, comprehensive, efficient, and effective selling system in the world today. I know that your business will benefit tremendously from applying its principles, as will mine.

Patrick C. Kelly
CEO
Physician Sales and Service

*(Mr. Kelly was elected to **Who's Who in Sales & Marketing in America**, and was chosen as **Healthcare Entrepreneur of the Year** for the State of Florida in 1990.)*

Preface

A woman walked into a psychologist's office lead-
ing a small white duck by a chain.

    "What can I do for you, madam?" the psychologist
asked.

    "Oh, it's not me," said the woman. "It's my hus-
band. He thinks he's a duck."

One of the interesting mysteries of life is the fact
that people can have such a wide range of perspectives on
identically the same phenomenon. Two people watching
the same movie, for instance, may have totally opposite
points of view about its meaning. Five people who witness the same automobile accident may report five diver-
gent accounts of what actually happened. Some juries become "hung" because jurors have different interpretations
of what they've heard from the people on the witness
stand.

    This book is about sales, and Lord knows there are
countless ideas on how to go about selling. Interestingly
enough, many of them are promoted as *the only way* to
sell, yet few of these approaches agree.

    It is our contention that the majority of selling
methodologies out there today tend to be variations of
each other—"chips off the same block," if you will—in
that they are all rooted in *old* economic conditions. This

book, on the other hand, is a totally *new* perspective because it grows out of current economic trends rather than from time-honored selling traditions.

Although there were legitimate reasons why those traditions were effective in the past, they no longer work as they once did. The truth is that there is a growing schism between yesterday's sales techniques and today's market conditions. Yet for lack of access to new and better skills, most salespeople as a matter of habit still try to do "business as usual" with methods that are "usual" in a world that is not.

Business is now changing at a hyperbolic rate. Loyalty is fast becoming a thing of the past in that customers move from one supplier to another without warning, remorse, or guilt.

It is commonly believed that nothing is more important in selling today than responding quickly to customer needs. Yet we will make the case that most current selling methodologies do *not* respond to the customer's *real* needs. More often, they direct the salesperson to naively *follow* the customer's lead—and we will explain how the customer's lead is designed to unconsciously divert the salesperson's attention away from the real problems, and invariably onto price. This is not to say, of course, that price is not an issue to the buyer; clearly it is. But while price is *an* issue, it is not *the* issue.

Selling is—as it always has been—the foundation

of our economy and the cornerstone of doing business. Selling makes the business world go 'round. As the world continues to change at a rate that no one could have previously imagined, it is imperative that the decision makers in our companies embrace these innovative selling strategies in order to excel in this new age.

We have written this book, therefore, not just for commissioned salespeople, who obviously are interested in *individual* profit, but also for executives and managers who must concern themselves with *corporate* profit in this frenzied, space-age economy in which we live.

This book is about Leadership Selling—that is, taking control of the selling interaction by *leading* the buyer away from price to his deeper buying motives. It is at these deeper levels where the potential for exceptional selling exists today.

Leadership Selling was conceived and incubated in our collective years of consulting experience that spans many years across multicultural and multinational lines. It evolved from our work with hundreds of CEOs, vice presidents of sales and marketing, and sales managers, not to mention training and developing untold thousands of aspiring salespeople.

We have worked successfully with nearly every industry imaginable, from oil-well leasing to HMOs, from government contracts to professional services, from financial planning to fire safety equipment, from real estate to information systems—we have, as the saying goes, "been there and done that," both in small companies and large. We have seen all the gimmicks that sales has to offer—the "tricks of the trade," if you will. We've had them used on us, and in days long gone, we've tried them ourselves, which is precisely how we know that they no longer work!

In short, Leadership Selling has been forged in the crucible of our own experience, first as salespeople ourselves and then as highly sought-after trainers in the selling profession at large. Because it grew to fruition "in the trenches," so to speak, rather than in some "ivory tower," two words that could be used to describe the effectiveness of Leadership Selling with absolute precision would be, *"It works!"* This fact above all else accounts for its inevitable and timely rise to world prominence as a selling system—one that has global application as well as universal appeal.

Two last thoughts. We speak in the masculine pronoun only because it is customary to do so; we certainly intend no sexism. And, since the words "product" and "services" are so often interchangeable, to save needless repetition of these words, we usually mean either or both whenever we refer to one or the other.

Jacksonville, Florida   *James M. Bleech*
                                      Dr. David G. Mutchler

Questions and Answers About the Book

Q: Who will benefit from reading *When the Other Guy's Price Is Lower*?

A: Obviously every *salesperson,* since they are the soldiers who are in the trenches and on the battle lines every day, fighting the good fight in the name of doing business. Also, *sales managers* and *vice presidents of sales and marketing,* the lieutenants who direct the soldiers in their daily selling warfare. And perhaps most importantly, *company owners, CEOs,* and *executives* who serve as the generals, and therefore who oversee—either directly or indirectly—the entire strategic selling operation.

Q: What's in it for me?

A: Increased sales, as well as higher levels of productivity, performance, and profit.

Q: Every sales book on the market says approximately the same thing. What's so different here?

A: You're quite right, most books on selling do make similar claims. By and large, however, readers who are well versed on the subject will know that such books aren't about something new in sales as much as they play the same old song on new and different instruments. *This, on the other hand, is a totally new song!*

Q: How is it new?

A: It's not about the subjects that you typically find in books about selling: giving better presentations, overcoming objections, doing better follow-up, making cold calls, establishing rapport, negotiating prices, and offering better value-added service. Instead, *it's about controlling the buyer/seller relationship from beginning to end by assuming and maintaining the leadership role.* Because taking on this leadership role is so vital to achieving consistently high sales results, we call the techniques that allow a salesperson to do so "Leadership Selling."

Q: Haven't salespeople generally thought they were in the leadership position with customers?

A: No doubt they have thought of themselves as leading the buyer in the sales transaction, but *thinking* that one is leading and *actually* leading are two quite different things. Historically, the vast majority of salespeople have believed they were leading by means of enthusiastically presenting features and benefits in order to persuade the customer to buy. The problem is that "convince-mode" selling tactics are ordinarily perceived as aggressive by customers, which in turn causes them to instinctively resist the seller's persuasive efforts.

Furthermore, the buyer's resistance is much more subtle than it is obvious, which makes it *extremely* powerful and difficult to overcome. It is similar to the Japanese art of jujitsu, where the strength and weight of an opponent are used against him. While salespeople have been accustomed to thinking that they are in the lead by giving fluent presentations, buyers have learned to cunningly use the information gathered in the presentation against the seller. In fact, the more information the customer can gain, the stronger his resistance becomes. So it is ironic that when the salesperson thinks he is leading the sales transaction, in reality he is doing little more than *following* the buyer's lead by playing directly into his hand.

Q: But haven't sales strategies of late become more sophisticated than just presenting features and benefits to the customer trying to persuade him to buy?

A: While the vast majority of salespeople still use feature and benefit selling as their primary approach, it is true that in the past few years there has been a gradual shift in the sales profession from convince-mode to "need-based" selling. This shift has occurred so that salespeople can recapture control of the sales call.

Q: What exactly do you mean by "need-based" selling?

A: "Need-based" selling can be found at the core of most popular selling systems in use today, although it appears in different forms under several different names. We use the term "need-based" in a very generic way, just as many people use the term "touch-tone" as a general reference to all tone-dialing telephones.

The premise of need-based selling is that customers buy in order to satisfy their needs. Therefore, salespeople are expected to ask questions to determine what the customer's needs are rather just present blindly. By doing so, a salesperson is perceived as being less persuasive and more inquisitive, which in effect reduces the buyer's resistance toward him. Once the seller is perceived as a consultative ally rather than an aggressive, high-pressured salesperson, he is in a much better position to "lead" the inter-action with his questions, and thereby control the sale.

Q: Is this what you mean by "Leadership Selling?"

A: Only minimally. We agree with the premise of need-based selling that the seller must regain the lead in the buyer/seller relationship, and that the principal tool at his disposal to accomplish this is to ask questions. We dis-agree, however, that people buy simply to satisfy their needs. Our contention is that when customers discuss their needs with salespeople, they are merely using com-fortable language to represent deeper and more substantial buying motives which, if revealed to the seller, would be emotionally painful for them to discuss.

In other words, when a salesperson interviews a buyer with the sole intention of determining his "needs," the seller has merely dented the surface in terms of uncover-ing the buyer's *real* motives, which are more *emotion*-based than need-based. Subsequently, the buyer is able to escape divulging his true buying intentions, thereby re-taining most of his control. Once this occurs, the seller has lost the lead to the buyer, and must revert back to giv-ing presentations and/or haggling about price.

Q: Are you saying that Leadership Selling goes *beyond* need-based selling—that is, it goes *deeper* in terms of discovering a buyer's true motives?

A: That's exactly what we're saying. Actually, Leader-ship Selling is not just a "selling system"; it is a "universal system of communication" *applied* to sales. It is universal in that, like music, it reaches down into the realm of human emotion where people live and breathe and *feel*, which is exactly the same space from which they buy.

The ability to lead customers past their awareness of surface needs to these deeper emotional reasons for buying *anything* represents ultimate control for salespeople in the buyer/seller relationship. Those who master the skills required to do so will gain an unquestionable competitive advantage in the marketplace, no small part of which is the increased efficiency with which they are able to identify the buyer's real motives.

Q: That given, what does Leadership Selling have to do with the title of the book, *When the Other Guy's Price Is Lower*?

A: Determining the customer's deeper buying motives requires specialized selling skills. This is because customers automatically resist salespeople by diverting attention away from their *real* problems, since the real problems can be painful to admit. This is precisely why buyers are so willing to discuss their "needs" and bicker about price—it protects them from delving into their painful feelings.

Leadership Selling helps you to efficiently and directly determine the customer's *deeper* buying motives, which again are always emotion-based. Once this is accomplished, it is relatively straightforward to sell him a solution because you've found the *real* problem as opposed to what the customer reports on the surface as merely his "need."

Q: So, are you saying that price isn't the real issue, just as need isn't the real issue?

A: Exactly! The problem is that because salespeople hear about price so often from their customers, they tend to believe that price really *is* the issue, just as they tend to believe that people buy to fulfill their needs. The truth is, from the buyer's perspective "price" and "need" are good bedfellows in that together they conspire to defend him against feeling his real reasons for buying.

Leadership Selling arms the salesperson to lead the customer through the maze of his own defenses to discover his emotional discomfort where actual buying decisions are made, instead of chasing after the buyer's decoys, namely, need and price. In doing so, the seller subsequently directs the buyer's attention away from price to his deeper buying motives, which is where the tremendous potential for increased profit lies today.

Part I

The Field of Play

PART I is a discussion of the dynamic economic forces at work in the selling profession today, forces that every salesperson and every company must come to grips with in order to successfully compete. Because the material in this section is philosophic and historical in nature, some readers may be tempted to jump ahead in their eagerness to utilize the practical strategies of Leadership Selling. Nevertheless, we strongly encourage reading PART I in its entirety before becoming immersed in the actual techniques of the system. This is because THE FIELD OF PLAY is both the backdrop from which Leadership Selling has emerged and the rationale by which it was destined to take center stage.

1

Sales and the Human Condition

To Be Human Is to Have Needs

In fact, to be *alive* is to have needs. But human needs are broader and deeper than the needs of other creatures, ranging from the simple to the complex, from the basic to the sublime.

Broadly defined, a need is the deficiency of something required, useful, or desired. Needs change from person to person and within each person from time to time.

They vary both in terms of intensity and scope. Needs are all-encompassing and permeate the entire human experience. From physical to psychological to spiritual needs; from family to fashion to privacy needs; from social to financial to educational needs—needs are ever-present and ever-changing in people's lives.

Unmet Needs Become "Problems"

Given that needs are so basic to life, human beings are perpetually in pursuit of attempting to get their needs met. And when needs are satisfied, people feel fulfilled.

However, in the time that elapses between need awareness and need fulfillment, some level of emotional discomfort results. Furthermore, the discomfort becomes a "problem" to the same degree that the *perceived* need remains unmet.

Problems "Seek" Solutions

Just as "nature abhors a vacuum," so do human beings detest feelings of emotional discomfort. The entirety of human life might be described as the ongoing effort, if not struggle, to resolve all such feelings—fear, anger, frustration, and the like. Single people seek primary relationships to resolve the loneliness that results from unfulfilled needs for love and companionship; medical scientists seek the cure for AIDS to resolve the anguish of those who are stricken with the dreaded disease; all people seek food to resolve their hunger, drink to resolve their thirst, and sleep to resolve their fatigue.

Unsatisfied needs are, in effect, problems looking for solutions. By and large, the pursuit of these solutions defines the human condition and, in the end, summarizes the primary motivating principle for all of life.

Solutions to Problems Sell

Examples that people "buy" solutions to their problems are endless. Indoor plumbing first sold because it replaced frequent trips to the well and the inconvenience of the outhouse; eyeglasses sold because they helped those whose vision was impaired to see better; spin-cycle washing machines sold to replace time-consuming wringer washers. From paper clips to computers, from fat-free foods to automobiles, from lawnmowers to compact discs, *all* products and services are purchased to solve problems at one level or another.

Profits Are Realized by Selling Solutions to Problems

What is important to note is that when solutions to problems sell, profits are realized. In 1927 Henry Ford received advanced orders for more than 375,000 cars before a single automobile was manufactured or delivered! Why did this happen? Because his Model A solved a major problem at that time: the industrial revolution made it necessary for the common man to find affordable transportation from his rural home into the cities to work.

These five principles, that (1) all people have needs, (2) unmet needs are emotionally problematic, (3) problems seek solutions, (4) people buy solutions to their

problems, and (5) profits are realized from selling those solutions, combine to form the definition and the purpose of all "business."

Moreover, human needs are forever changing. Therefore, people are perpetual consumers in their quest for solutions to their problems—which, again, is the equivalent of saying that people never cease trying to resolve their emotional pain. This fact is *extremely* important for salespeople to understand. It is the foundation upon which the remainder of this book is built, and will play a major role in outselling the competition "when the other guy's price is lower." It is, in essence, the alpha and the omega of *all* sales.

2

The Changing Lens of the Buyer

1995, Someplace in Iowa

It is almost corn-harvesting time, and Pete walks up and down the rows of his corn, hand-picking the ears that have ripened early. He plans to take them to the nearest town to test the market before harvesting the remainder of his crop. Pete tosses each ear into a wheelbarrow, and as he comes to the end of a row, he dumps them into the bed of his pickup truck.

It is 92° and humid, Pete is sweaty and covered

with dust, and he is exhausted from the heat. When he finally fills the truck, he heads for the nearest town five miles away.

As he approaches the grain mill, he notices a blackboard with the price of corn written on it: $4.65 per bushel. Pete is stunned, since he was anticipating at least $8.00 per bushel for his corn.

Figure 1

In total disbelief, he walks in and asks the buyer, "How much are you paying for corn?" The buyer responds, "Just as it says on the blackboard, four sixty-five." "But sir, that's not nearly enough," Pete replies. "And besides, you haven't seen my presentation yet." Having nothing better to do at the moment, the buyer agrees to listen to Pete's story.

Hoping for a higher price, Pete hurries out to his pickup, grabs his briefcase, slide projector, and foam presentation boards in preparation to educate the buyer as to what makes his corn worth more than $4.65 per bushel. He is very proud of his elaborate presentation, having invested $25,000 with a marketing firm that helped him develop a first-class sales pitch.

And the Show Begins

Pete flashes up high-quality slides and foamboards that demonstrate that he is different from any other farmer out there, and that his corn is worth more than anyone else's because he runs a premiere operation. He explains that he has spent the last two years implementing a complete program of Total Quality Management, and that he has nothing but top-quality inspectors whose job it is to ensure that the corn is grown to every specification.

Pete mentions also that he has made it a policy to use only American-built equipment and that he will not hire any illegal alien labor. He emphasizes that he has earned a Ph.D. in agronomy, and that he has all of his employees enrolled in continuing education programs in order to keep them abreast of the latest agricultural developments.

He explains further that he uses computers to track all of the various accounting and business information; that he has satellite and television systems that keep him up-to-date on various weather changes; and that he has the most extensive preventative maintenance programs for all of his equipment. He has all of this information documented on slide after slide and picture board after picture board.

Pete has rehearsed his presentation over and over again, and he is very proficient in his delivery. He finishes the forty-five minute talk, then turns to the corn buyer and asks, "Now, sir, how much will you pay me for my corn?" And the corn buyer, even though he is impressed by what just occurred, answers, "Same as before, four sixty-five per bushel."

Pete is infuriated by the buyer's response. He throws his material into a box and storms out the door. He mutters to himself, "This uneducated fool just doesn't understand what my business is all about; I'm going to drive to the next town to see if I can get a higher price from someone who does understand."

He cranks his air conditioner to high and drives sixty-three miles to the nearest town. He looks until he finds the grain elevator—and, to his dismay, there at the entrance is another blackboard with exactly the same words written on it: "$4.65 per bushel."

Pete's problem is that he is trying to sell a product that has become a commodity. A commodity is any product or service that can be obtained easily because its supply exceeds the demand for it.

What happens in a commodity market is that, because a product is in abundant supply, its price slides downward until it hits rock bottom. Thereafter, two factors make it extremely difficult to generate profit. First, the price of the product is now relatively fixed because the supply exceeds the demand. Second, the cost of doing business is driven up due to added expenses—in Pete's case, driving time, presentation time, the cost of gasoline, and so on. These two factors in combination—that is, fixed prices and increasing costs—have the negative effect of *decreasing* profits overall.

This same phenomenon happens to individual companies and to entire industries, just as it does with products. But that's a discussion for a different time. Let's focus here on what this means specifically about sales.

The Natural Life Cycle of Every Product and Service

All products and services from the day of their inception slide predictably to a commodity status, from high price/high profit to low price/low profit. This happens as a result of the product passing naturally through the three stages of its life cycle—stages that are necessary, predictable, and inevitable. Virtually *nothing* can be done in a supply and demand economy to stop this slide from happening.

The Commodity Slide

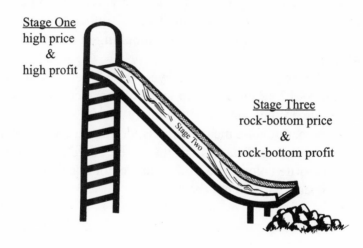

Figure 2

Stage One

Once a product is developed that is perceived by the consumer as solving his problem, then assuming that the product is marketed, a demand naturally ensues. People flock to purchase the new "solution" to their problem, just as they did in 1927 when Henry Ford introduced the first Model A.

The primary characteristic in a stage-one market is that the demand for a product exceeds its supply. From the manufacturer's perspective, the first challenge is to market the product to increase consumer awareness and thereby create the demand. The second goal is to duplicate, that is, mass produce the product so that it can be made available to the many interested buyers.

As for the psychology of the buyer, in stage one of a product's life cycle the consumer is acutely aware of his problem. Consequently, he is eager to purchase the product in the hope of solving that problem. Since there are few competitors at this point, he rarely gets the opportunity to ask, "Which *one* shall I buy?"; other choices are simply not yet available. The compelling question on his mind is, "*How* can I get one?"

In stage one of its life cycle the Model A, you will recall, sold like hotcakes, in spite of the fact that it was available in only one color, namely black. People who were desperate for a means of transportation to get to work didn't wait to purchase a car until they could buy one in their favorite color. The truth is that color wasn't even an issue because it was not the problem.

Stage Two

Over time, more and more companies enter the market to fill the demand created in stage one. As supply increases and begins to approach demand, each competing company starts to feel the others' presence through shared sales. As this occurs, companies attempt to gain the selling advantage by differentiating their products in some salable way. The result: consumers begin to have options that were previously not available to them.

As supply began to catch up with demand in the automobile industry, for instance, the Reo Motor Car

Company—along with other competitors—started mass producing cars in colors *other than* black. This unique selling feature, along with other improvements, meant that the interested consumer was suddenly introduced to new choices in his car-shopping experience.

This fact—that options emerge in stage two of a product's life cycle—causes a subtle but important shift to occur in the mind of the buyer. His attention moves from *"How* do I get it?" to *"Which* product is the best one for me?" This change in focus from "how?" to "which one?" automatically moves the buyer's awareness *away from his problem* to be solved and *onto the choices* that are available to him.

Example: Imagine two people in separate automobiles traveling across the United States. One is on the West Coast headed east, the other is on the East Coast headed west. They both left at 7:00 a.m., and as noontime approaches, both are hungry, and both plan to eat lunch within the hour.

The person traveling east is heading into the desert and knows that the next town has one and only one restaurant—the last to be found for hundreds of miles. He has heard that the restaurant in question serves only one entree. He is likely thinking, "I'm hungry, and I'm going to eat at the next restaurant because it's my last opportunity to do so for several hours." He is focused on his need to eat, and plans to meet that need with the only available meal. He is *not* concerned about the fact that there won't be the usual menu of foods from which to choose.

The person headed west, on the other hand, is fifteen miles from the next major city. He knows that there will be hundreds of eating establishments to choose from, and that he has his pick of places to go to and foods to eat. Unlike the first person, he is thinking, "What would I like to eat for lunch, and where?" Because the second person has options that the first one doesn't, his attention is focused on an entirely different matter—namely, on his eating options rather than on his hunger pains.

~

The point, again, is that *the more aware the buyer becomes of his options, the less aware he becomes of the problem that prompted his desire to purchase in the first place.*

Stage Three

In time, the window of opportunity for competing companies to modify and fine-tune their products and services narrows tremendously. Consider the following scenario.

Company A makes powdered laundry detergent and promotes it on its improved cleaning power. Companies B and C do the same. Company A adds bleach to make the clothes whiter. Company B adds bleach plus a fresh scent. Company C adds bleach, a fresh scent, and in addition makes it ultra-concentrated. Company A develops detergent that cleans well, whitens clothes, adds a fresh scent, is ultra-concentrated, and is biodegradable. Company B matches that, but throws in a soap scoop for easier measuring. Not to be outdone, Company C does the same, except it puts a handle on the box. Company A then makes a stronger handle, and so on, seemingly without end.

This is typical of stage three in a product's life cycle. Supply has equaled or exceeded demand, and, as a result, there are countless nearly-indistinguishable choices available to the consumer.

The next logical step for competing companies to gain the selling advantage, then, is to lower their prices. As a result, and as could be expected, the customer's attention moves automatically to the price issue.

In other words, the buyer's awareness has evolved from "*How* do I get one?" (stage one) to "*Which* is the best one for me?" (stage two) to "How do I get one for the *lowest price*, given that they all so closely resemble one another?" (stage three). When this final shift occurs, the product has become a true commodity. It is in such common supply that price has become the most important issue, which, you will recall from Pete and his corn, is the definition of a commodity market.

Something else has happened, too. In stage three, yet another layer of insulation has developed that separates the consumer from his awareness of the problem or need that motivated him to shop in the first place. He now has a growing number of price options that cause his attention to shift even further away from his original problem. As a result, he is able to manipulate the salesperson into believing that the only real concern on his mind is price, thus masking the underlying problem that drives him to buy.

All products and services are the solution to some problem. However, as they slide inevitably and predictably from stage one in their natural life cycle to stage three, they become increasingly abundant and, therefore, increasingly a commodity. The more a product or service becomes a commodity, the more the consumer's attention becomes focused on price, and the less aware he becomes of the problem that initially motivated him to buy.

~

    Needless to say, all of this has a profound impact on selling. When the computer was in stage one of its life cycle, for example, IBM established itself as the clear leader by mass producing computers for business use. The salesperson's job was little more than to be an order-taker. Once the computer was brought to the attention of the people who needed it, the product basically sold itself.

    In stage two, as supply approached demand, Apple entered the market and differentiated itself by concentrating its efforts on developing the personal computer (PC) for home use. Soon thereafter, IBM moved into the PC market. Computer sales necessarily took on a new complexion in that salespeople now had to present the features and benefits of their respective computers, thereby trying to convince the prospective buyer that "My computer is the best one for you."

    Almost immediately, one competitor after another entered the race and flooded the market with IBM "compatibles." Down came the prices (stage three), and thus the computer quickly became a commodity. And, in spite of the fact that computer technology is still expanding faster than anyone can keep up with, price has nevertheless become the primary issue on nearly every user's mind.

    One of the natural consequences of a commodity market is that it places tremendous power in the hands of the buyer. As price becomes the focus of the sales transaction, consumers are positioned to negotiate lower and lower prices by "shopping around," pitting one company against the other.

This maddening situation, where buyers are preoccupied with price rather than with buying a product to solve their original problem, is where so many businesses and salespeople find themselves today. It is precisely this state of affairs that calls the question which this book is intended to answer, namely, "When the other guy's price is lower, *how* can you still make the sale?"

One answer is to be a true commodity player. This means that you purposely *intend* to become the lowest-cost provider and sell your product for the lowest price. The only way this can work to maintain profit in the long run, of course, is to ensure that your company can manufacture the product for the lowest cost while maintaining high-volume sales.

The problem with this approach is that it is limited to those select few companies that can actually win the low-cost manufacturing war. For the majority of businesses that can't do so, although many of them literally "die" trying, striving to become a true commodity provider is clearly not a viable option.

As companies and their sales representatives cave in to inevitable price pressures from the buyer, prices tend to spiral downward, and profit margins shrink. For many companies it becomes a blood bath, turning into a desperate struggle just to survive. Many of them sink into red ink, and eventually go bankrupt. The attempt to gain price advantage grows into a monster that gradually swallows them up. Again, this is because in a stage-three or commodity market the customer can dictate the terms, often winning "hands down!"

In the end, this lowest-cost/highest-volume strategy for all but the small minority of companies that actually achieve it only begs the question of *how* to make the sale when the other guy's price is lower. The deeper meaning of that question, then, and the real purpose of this book, is: "When the other guy's price is lower *and you choose not to be the lowest-priced player in the game*, **how** can you still make the sale?"

3

Customer Service
to the Rescue?

For most companies, then, the attempt to gain market share in a commodity market through price advantage is time-limited. Prices can only sink so low before discounting has to stop if a company hopes to remain in business. But if lowering the price is no longer an option, then what is?

There's a New Game in Town

The answer for the majority of businesses, of course, is customer service, which by now is a "household" word in nearly every industry.

Customer service, we all know, involves "going the extra mile" for the consumer in ways that are intended to "one-up" the competition. It includes such things as value-added service—i.e., giving the customer more for his money, serving the customer in general after the sale, and of particular importance, ensuring rapid delivery time.

The trouble is that what one company does for its customers in the name of value-added service is soon copied by its competitors. In time, all the competing companies' service, as with their prices, begin to look more and more alike.

Consider delivery time as an example of how this principle works. Let's say that Company A can deliver its products in 24 hours, whereas a competitor—Company B—can deliver them in 18 hours. Company B uses this as a selling advantage, and attracts customers away from Company A. In order to compete, Company A shaves its delivery time to 12 hours. Company B gets it down to 10 hours; and so on. The point comes where the difference in delivery time between one company and another is miniscule, and is therefore insignificant. When all is said and done, who cares whether the product arrives in 45 minutes or 40 minutes? At some point, continuing to improve it borders on sheer insanity.

There are, of course, many other examples that could be used. Company ABC supplies its customers the value-added service of a computer system to help inventory their products. Not to be outdone, companies EFG, HIJ, and KLM soon follow. Company EFG offers value-added technical support. In order to compete, so must companies ABC, HIJ, and KLM, and so on.

The Point

In time, customer service is subject to *exactly the same* dynamics as occurs with product differentiation and price advantage. That is, all the competing companies not only begin to look the same, sound the same, and cost the same, they also *service their customers in the same way*! In effect, **customer service itself slides to commodity status.**

While it is true that salespeople who represent companies with superior customer service can thereby gain the selling edge at least temporarily, it is also true in a commodity market that buyers can leverage customer service to their distinct advantage. The consumer can say to a salesperson, "Look, I can buy from either you or from Joe at the same price, so what more can you do for me so that you can make the sale?"

This question represents a "you need me more than I need you," or maybe more accurately, a "you owe me" attitude on the buyer's part that can only happen in the context of a commodity market. The fact that the product is a commodity is what allows him to ask this question at all.

Value-Added Service Has a Price Tag

You've probably heard the saying in business that "there's no such thing as a free lunch." So it is with customer service. Directly or indirectly, sooner or later, value-added service increases a company's cost of doing business. "Free" computer systems, "free" seminars, "free" consulting—all such services require either capital outlay or people's time, the costs for which must be subtracted from the bottom line.

Add to this the truism that "the more one gets, the more one wants." Translated to business, this means that the more service a company gives to its customers, the more service their customers expect and demand. The result is a bottomless pit into which an endless stream of costly customer favors can fall.

"Value-Added" Is Therefore an Illusion

Remember, customer service matures as a selling strategy in a commodity market where prices *cannot* be reduced any further if a company hopes to remain profitable. Yet, since companies must cover the expense of delivering value-added services, it is ironic that service costs are necessarily charged back to the consumer. This is accomplished, not directly by charging openly for the service per se, but indirectly by discreetly raising prices over time for the product. It is precisely because every competing company must do the same that the *appearance* is given to consumers that prices are stable, since everyone's price by comparison still seems to be about the same.

The truth is, even though there is much commotion in the business world today about the importance of offering value-added services, customer service as a *selling advantage* has nearly run its course. Intuitively, consumers know this because service, having become a commodity itself, can now be taken for granted. As a result, consumers attempt to move the playing field back to price where their ultimate power lies.

If salespeople are going to be honest with themselves, they will have to admit that the battle they face daily in the field is one between the salesperson trying to justify value-added service versus the customer who, like a broken record, hammers away at price, price, price. At some level there is wisdom in the consumer's position because, after all is said and done, customer service costs money and is therefore still about price.

This is why value-added service is not the ultimate answer, just as duplication, differentiation, and price negotiation were not. What must happen instead is for the salesperson to redirect the buyer's attention away from price onto a different subject, one that in the end will prove to be the *real* issue in the buyer/seller game. In order to accomplish this, salespeople must proactively *lead* rather than reactively follow the buyer. It is only appropriate, therefore, that we have named this new approach "Leadership Selling."

4

Enter Warp-Speed Change

While an hour is an hour is an hour in that it is still sixty minutes on the clock, in the world of business an hour—like the old gray mare—just "ain't what she used to be." The culprit is an information explosion triggered by radical advancements in technology that together are changing the very definition of time, and sales.

There was a day when information spread slowly. The printing press was invented in the 15th century, but it wasn't developed sufficiently to mass produce books until the mid-1800s. Radio didn't come on the scene until the early 1900s, and television not until the mid-1900s. Socially, politically, economically—in all facets of life, people were generally uninformed as to how the rest of the world lived. As a result, change occurred slowly.

In business, therefore, competition didn't just magically arise overnight. Nothing changed that fast. Consider, for example, that the first steam engine was built in 1712. No major modifications occurred until 1769. And it wasn't until 1860—*one hundred and forty-eight years later*—that the successor to the steam engine—the gas-fueled internal combustion engine—was developed!

The point is that it took considerable time for change to occur. Generations passed before potential competitors were able to learn enough about another company's products to replicate them. As a general rule, products had a fairly long life expectancy, and competing companies had ample time to gain market advantage in one or more of a product's life stages.

But Times Have Changed

As technology has steadily advanced through the ages, however, the effect has been a gradual increase in the rate at which information flows, and therefore, in the rate at which change occurs.

For example, in 1800, a letter sent coast to coast in this country could easily take months by stagecoach to reach its destination; in 1860, several weeks by pony express; after 1869, a week or so by train; in 1920, a few days by plane; in 1960, overnight by jet; since the mid-1980s, a few seconds via fax machines; and most recently, instantaneous communication through e-mail, plus same-day delivery of hard copy information anywhere in the continental United States!

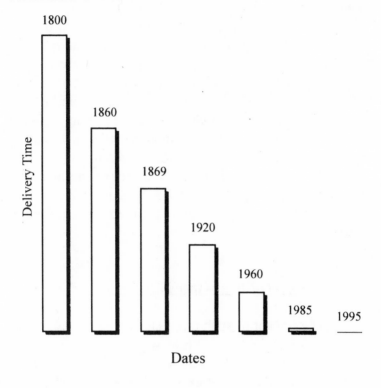

Figure 3

Technology is advancing so rapidly today that information is globally accessible at lightning speed. Product designs, manufacturing secrets, and marketing strategies are becoming increasingly a matter of public domain. For all intents and purposes, nearly all information is now at the fingertips of anyone who wants it. Copy machines, computers, satellite communications, on-line computer services—these and similar technologies have all moved in the direction of reducing the length of time that any company can protect the ownership of its trade secrets.

The truth is that technology has reached warp speed. "The future" is no longer perceived as generations away, or even years away. *Warp-speed change is fast bringing the future to the very doorstep of today.*

The consequence is that the time required for one company to clone another company's products is exponentially faster than ever before. As a result, the life expectancy of products and services is being shortened to ridiculously brief periods of time. Not uncommonly, marketing brochures are outdated before they come off the press. Anyone who owns a computer will know that the system they purchased three, two, or even one month ago is already becoming obsolete. The fact of the matter is that the length of time that it takes for a product to move through its life cycle has been reduced to a microfraction of what it once was.

The Effect of Warp-Speed Change on Selling

The impact of such rapid change on the sales process is unprecedented. While we have discussed the stages of a product's life cycle in Chapter 2 as it relates to the *buyer*, we have not yet examined those same stages as it relates to the *seller*. This will be necessary to do next in order to understand the full effect of warp-speed change on the selling profession.

Stage-One Selling: To Market, to Market...

It is really a misnomer to say that "selling" is what happens in the initial stage of a new product where the demand is high and the supply is scarce. In actuality, if the product is successfully marketed—which means that customers know *of its existence* and *where to buy it*—the job of the "salesperson" is relatively straightforward. The emphasis on selling the product is on advertising it, which is accomplished through several "tried and true" methods such as television commercials, radio spots, billboards, newsprint, magazine ads, and various avenues of direct mail pieces. In addition, advertising agencies create catchy slogans and jingles in the hope of drawing an audience to the new product.

Once a product is adequately marketed, it tends to sell itself. The "salesperson" has little more to do than make the sales call and take the order. The fact that the seller has a pleasant personality can be a valuable bonus, but the real skills required in stage one amount to the basic functions of recording pertinent information and, where appropriate, delivering the product. Again, in stage one the customer perceives the product as the *only* solution to his problem. No real "selling" strategies are required, since under these circumstances the product is in such high demand that the sale is practically guaranteed.

Stage-Two Selling: The Advent of Show and Tell

In the evolving product-differentiated market, new selling skills are required in order to keep products moving. It is no longer effective simply to introduce something new by saying, "Here it is," and assume that customers will automatically flock to buy it. Because of the growing number of competing products in the marketplace, it now becomes necessary to inform customers as to "what makes this one *better* than the other guy's."

It would be a mistake, in other words, to assume that those who make buying decisions automatically know what makes one competing product better than another. In spite of the fact that marketing efforts usually increase at this juncture to help point out product differences, personal contact between the buyer and the manufacturer is required to fully demonstrate what makes each product unique, as well as beneficial, to him. A "go-between" person who represents the company and explains product differences to the customer is now needed, which is more in the spirit of what we know as a "salesperson" today.

Whether in retail, door-to-door, or business-to-business sales, salespeople in a stage-two market need a way to do battle with the competition, and win. Armed with a superior product, or at least with the *belief* that they are so armed, it is essential that salespeople begin to sing the praises of their wares.

Their job is to convince the prospective buyer that the features and benefits of product X over product Y make it worth buying. Feature-benefit selling becomes the modus operandi—or feature-advantage-benefit (FAB) selling, as some prefer to call it—where "presentations" are given to customers to "educate" them about why this is the "best of all possible products" amidst the growing number of choices available.

By and large, feature-benefit selling, or "show-and-tell" as we often call it, is an effective sales methodology in a stage-two, product-differentiated market. Salespeople generally know far more about their products than their customers do. And customers are generally eager to hear how the products will benefit them. They welcome the sales presentation as an informative and educational experience. As we said, their question is no longer "*How* can I get one?" as is true in stage one, but "*Which* is the best one for me?"

Assuming that the salesperson has valid reasons as to why the customer should make the purchase, and assuming that the price is competitive, "convince-mode" (i.e. feature-benefit) selling is a relatively effective way to sell the product. If someone can purchase Brand X for $25 or Brand Y for $25, and Brand X has three more features and benefits than Brand Y, this is an easy decision to make.

In stage two, the keys to successful selling are acquiring an abundance of product knowledge with which to educate the buyer, and solid presentation skills. A charming personality with a healthy dose of enthusiasm certainly doesn't hurt, of course. But these individual characteristics often aren't necessary, since in a purely product-differentiated market, products tend to sell themselves once their unique differences and their obvious advantages are understood by the customer.

Stage-Three Selling: The Price Is Right, or Is It?

Remember, stage three in a product's life cycle is a commodity market. Supply exceeds demand, so the product is readily available. Again, the customer's concern moves from "how" to "which one" to "which is the lowest priced."

Consequently, in stage three the selling game changes to a new set of rules where the customer tries to buy for the least amount possible while the salesperson tries to sell for the largest margin of profit. That given, the sales approach in stage three necessarily moves to the sophisticated art of negotiations.

Actually, there are two types of commodity-market negotiations: one where salespeople still have direct contact with the customer—which is the majority of the time; and the other, where there is no more opportunity for personal contact between the salesperson and the customer. When direct contact is possible, price negotiation can be impersonal if not ruthless, which is problematic in a profession where it is so important to maintain ongoing relationships.

As a selling strategy, therefore, face-to-face negotiation requires that a personal touch be added to an otherwise cold and heartless process; hence the emphasis moves to developing "people skills." Techniques like the following become important:

- establishing rapport
- reading body language
- controlling attitude and mood
- communicating effectively
- influencing people
- presenting enthusiastically
- memorizing names
- creating desire
- overcoming objections
- closing the sale

In those cases where there is no further possibility for personal contact with the customer, improving written communication skills is the one remaining strategy to increase sales, since any attempt at communication in this instance is a one-way street. But this only happens in an *extreme* commodity market which, because it is the exception rather than the rule, is a subject for another time.

"Stage Four": Selling Customer Service

At the point where prices of competing products are approximately the same, those salespeople who offer the greatest customer service programs have a distinct selling advantage over their competitors. We have already discussed the liabilities of selling customer service, namely that the more people get, the more they want, and that sooner or later the issue necessarily reverts back to price.

Nevertheless, in the interim, while a company has a clear lead over its competitors in the customer service arena, it is indeed possible to increase sales using service as a selling ploy. To do so simply requires stage-two selling tactics—that is, presenting the features and benefits of one's customer service programs, with emphasis on the ways that your services are better than what your competition offers.

Now that we've discussed the three stages of a product's life cycle from the *seller's* perspective—or four, if one includes customer service—the reader can better understand the full impact of warp-speed change on the sales process.

The problem is that the length of time that it takes to move through each stage of a product's life cycle is shrinking so fast that the selling advantage inherent in each stage is shrinking accordingly. It is diminishing so fast, in fact, that there is very little time in any single stage to outsell the competition using any of the traditional selling approaches. Subsequently, it is increasingly difficult to capture the selling advantage in any one of the four life stages.

None of this is to say that salespeople can dismiss the importance of traditional selling methodologies related to each of a product's life stages. As long as there are human beings, there will be creative genius in the form of new inventions and better ideas to manufacture and sell. Once those ideas materialize into a product or service for which there is a demand, the first selling priority will continue to be marketing the product and making it available. This will be followed by presenting features and benefits of the improved products, then by negotiating price, and finally by selling value-added service. The issue is, rather, that while this cycle used to take decades to complete, and then years, many products complete the entire cycle now in a matter of months and sometimes even weeks!

An Example

A specific situation that recently happened in one industry exemplifies this point well. Approximately one year ago an instrument was developed and made available for in-office pregnancy tests that took about one hour to determine the results. Since then, through five different manufacturers, the time required to perform the test has dropped from one hour to thirty minutes, to ten minutes, to five minutes, to one minute, to only a matter of seconds!

Each company believed that it had the technological advantage to finally capture the market and dominate sales. Imagine all of the highly-charged sales meetings that undoubtedly took place to celebrate each breakthrough, all of the brochures that were rewritten to announce the latest technology, all of the revisions of price lists, and all of the hours of new product training. Yet in spite of the excitement and anticipation of each new breakthrough, the selling advantage lasted *at most* two months for each of the manufacturers because the product was practically obsolete before it hit the market!

In Summary

While a company is destined in a supply and demand economy to go through the various selling stages with every new product, *competing companies are follow-*

ing suit more and more quickly, making it difficult to sustain a competitive advantage. The net effect is the narrowing of opportunity for any company to gain market dominance, resulting in more competitors—and therefore more and more salespeople—sharing smaller and smaller pieces of a finite pie.

It is therefore impossible for salespeople today—*except in very rare circumstances*—to achieve or maintain a competitive advantage through any of the traditional selling methodologies. Such strategies are old, outdated, and they don't work as well as they once did. Sure, it is still possible to sell using these techniques; people obviously do it every day, since nothing happens in business until something is sold. But that's not the issue. It isn't a question of whether one *can* sell today using worn-out methods. The issue is that none of the old selling approaches give one a decided advantage in the warp-speed marketplace. The vast majority of salespeople struggle day after day using techniques that are simply obsolete.

To make matters worse, most salespeople *continue to sell the way they learned to sell* when they first entered the profession. The selling strategies that they learned, of course, correlated to the stage that their product was in at the time. Because they were successful to some degree using such techniques, their selling behaviors were positively reinforced. As a result, those behaviors became permanent habits that for many have not changed, even though the marketplace has changed dramatically.

In our view, and as an aside, this is why motivational sales training has become so popular in recent years. It is a shot of adrenaline for salespeople who need a "boost." Many salespeople are emotionally battered and bruised, and they are exhausted. Why? Because, like a computer technician forced to repair a circuit board with a crowbar, the selling techniques that have served the profession so well in the past are simply behind the economic times that dominate the market today.

While motivational speeches delivered by sales gurus can be helpful in the short run, what salespeople are *really* hungry for is a new way of approaching sales, given that warp-speed change has become a fact of life.

Therefore, the real question becomes, *"Is there a better way?"* The answer: absolutely yes! What selling needs now is not another bandage, but a major operation. That is, it needs a completely new way to conceptualize the selling process, one that both acknowledges and works in harmony with the economic realities of warp-speed change. Leadership Selling is a communication system that provides the solution to exactly these objectives.

5

Back to Basics

Most successful coaches when confronted with the frustration of defeat have instinctively reverted to a "back to basics" approach with their team. In football this means focusing on blocking and tackling drills; in basketball, emphasizing passing and shooting techniques; in baseball, concentrating on catching and hitting skills. Yet it is not just in athletics but in all facets of life—sales included—that the "back to basics" principle holds true: *winning is invariably the result of practicing and perfecting the fundamentals.*

However, there is a major difference between sales and athletics in terms of what constitutes "the basics." Ask ten salespeople or sales managers how they would define the basics of selling, and you will more than likely hear ten different answers.

Again, there are two reasons why this is true. First, many of them are still selling the way they learned to sell—and were rewarded for it—in years past. Second, each stage of a product's life cycle requires different "basics," and what stage a product is in at any given time heavily influences one's definition. In stage one, for example, "back to basics" entails sharpening one's marketing and order-taking skills; in stages two and four, presentation skills; and in stage three, negotiation and people skills.

The Problem in Sales Is That Most Definitions of "Basics" Have Become Outdated

In years past, change occurred slowly, and there was ample time in each of a product's life stages to perfect the "basics." Now that warp-speed change is upon us, this has become nearly impossible to do. Each stage is here and gone so fast that one barely has time to *practice* his skills, let alone *perfect* them. What is needed now is a new definition of "basics."

The five principles introduced in Chapter 1 are precisely that definition. They form the foundation upon which Leadership Selling is built. Notice as you review them that they are not about products as much as they are about people, not about facts as much as feelings, not about external factors as much as internal factors. In essence, the definition of "basics" in Leadership Selling is grounded in the nature of the human condition—that is, in the psychological makeup of the buyer conjoined with the very meaning and purpose of sales.

Those five principles, you will recall, are:

1. **All people have needs.**
2. **Unmet needs become problems.**
3. **Problems seek solutions.**
4. **People buy solutions to their problems.**
5. **Profits are realized from selling solutions.**

Every sale *without exception* is undergirded by these five basic principles. The trouble is that the four stages of supply and demand economics conspire to progressively turn the buyer's attention *away from* his initial problem *onto* the increasing number of product and customer service options, and ultimately onto price.

Since people always purchase solutions to their problems, price—while indeed *an* issue—is not the most important issue, in spite of the fact that the buyer would like the salesperson to believe otherwise.

It is vital, therefore, that the salesperson becomes highly skilled at "leading" the buyer back to his true buying motive, namely to his original underlying problem. To do so requires specific leadership skills, which again is why we call this "Leadership Selling."

Technically speaking, Leadership Selling is not

merely a "selling system," per se. It would be more accurate to describe it as a "universal system of problem solving" in that it is effective for communicating across a much broader spectrum of situations than just in sales. Because of this, many people we've worked with have reported how much Leadership Selling has helped them resolve problems in their personal and social lives, as well.

Ultimately, the reason this is true is because the techniques of Leadership Selling reach deeper than mere human "need," which is where so many selling systems place the primary emphasis with customers today. Instead they descend into the "emotional zone" where people's true motives lie. It is here that the potential for highly efficient sales can be found, regardless of the product or service being sold. And make no mistake about it, sales *efficiency* may well be the single most important factor for effective selling now that warp-speed change is here to stay.

This Approach Creates a Clear Challenge for Salespeople

Becoming a leader who takes total control of the sales call and helps the customer shift his attention back to his problem is no small undertaking, and it requires unique and specialized skills. This is because, as a general rule, buyers—like all human beings—don't enjoy being made aware of their problems, hence they resist the salesperson's efforts toward that end.

Therefore, a commitment and a certain level of discipline are necessary to learn and develop these Leadership Selling skills, which will be discussed in much detail in Part IV. The main point here is that even though this approach takes salespeople time to fully learn and implement, their reward in terms of increased sales begins almost immediately, and grows proportionately as they continue to practice and polish these skills.

Clearly, the development of the Leadership Selling skills that follow is the wave of the future in sales. Those salespeople who hone them are destined to become the uncontested leaders in their respective industries. This is due principally to the efficiency with which they learn to diffuse the price issue by identifying a buyer's true motives, and subsequently are able to secure the sale.

In addition, Leadership Selling promises to earn much more respect for salespeople who implement it, elevating them to a new level of professionalism in the eyes of the often-cynical buyer.

Don't be alarmed if the skills involved appear difficult in the beginning, since they represent a radical shift from how most selling occurs today. Once the conceptual transition takes place in the mind of the salesperson that selling is not about *price* nearly so much as it is about discovering the buyer's underlying *problems,* mastering the techniques of Leadership Selling becomes relatively straightforward and largely a matter of practice.

Part II

The Players

If anything is more important than to "Know Thyself," it is to "Know Thine Enemy," as all successful leaders surely understand. While sales isn't an obvious "battle" in the classic sense of the word—in fact, it is often referred to as a "dance"—at a deeper psychological level sales is out-and-out warfare between seller and buyer. PART II: THE PLAYERS is an eye-opening examination of the subtle dynamics in operation between these two opposing forces, and why the salesperson must consequently change the way he goes to battle if he truly hopes to win.

6

Buyers *Hold* Their Cards

We usually don't think of consumers as having a process, or a system, that they rely on for making a buying decision. But buyers *do* have a system, and a very tight-fisted one at that! Their system has become instinctive and automatic, having evolved in the collective unconscious of the consumer over hundreds of years of buying experiences. It has been refined to the point that it is almost impenetrable unless and until the salesperson understands both its source and its power.

Why the Need for a Buyer's Process?

In order to gain something of value, the buyer must also relinquish something of value, namely his money. He assumes some risk, therefore, whenever he makes a purchase; the higher his capital outlay, the greater his risk.

One risk involves whether the value of what the buyer is gaining is equal to or greater than the money he's willing to give up. The buyer innately distrusts the seller because they have different and opposite motives. The buyer's motive is to get the best value for his investment; the seller's is to make the most profit. The buyer's process, therefore, serves the purpose of protecting him against his fear of not getting his money's worth and of giving up more of his assets and resources than is absolutely necessary. Understandably, he approaches the buyer/seller interaction cautiously (buyer beware!), and tries to control it at every turn.

The Buyer's Process

Buyers employ a carefully crafted four-step approach that has been forged unconsciously over time into a highly-efficient system that helps them establish the dominant position in order to maintain a feeling of control.

Step One

Once a buyer has an interest in a particular product or service, his first strategy is to hold his cards as closely to his chest as possible so that the seller can't see them. Since information is power, he must withhold as much information from the seller as he possibly can. This is accomplished in several different ways:

- don't offer any more information than is absolutely necessary;

- if asked a question, evade the real answer in any way possible;

- use the phrase "I'm just looking" to throw the salesperson off track;

- when all else fails, tell a white lie.

The point is that the buyer's perception of salespeople is far from pretty. We occasionally do an exercise with salespeople in which we ask them for as many descriptive terms for the word "salesperson" as they can think of in thirty seconds. Answers we commonly hear include: smooth talker, fast talker, pushy, overbearing, high-pressured, silver-tongued, gift of gab, deceitful, assuming, polyester suit, aggressive, untrustworthy, liar, exaggerator, and charlaton—not exactly the profile of an individual that we'd like our sons and daughters to grow up to be!

In spite of the fact that only a very small percentage of salespeople actually fit this image, *all* salespeople must face the fact that this is how they are generally *perceived* by the buyer. Somehow the "snake oil" image of the salesperson lives on as a projection of the buyer's worst fears, namely that he may lose control and be taken advantage of by the seller. To prevent these fears from coming true, withholding information and lying as a means of self-defense is sanctioned, and commonplace.

It's interesting that there are a few scenarios in our culture where lying is the socially acceptable, even *expected,* thing to do. One of those occurs in the buying situation. "White lies" that are told to salespeople by buyers seem to be forgiven in the name of self-protection, just as it's okay to tell a bully who's stalking your child that "he isn't home right now," even though he's really hiding under the bed!

Step Two

The buyer's central question—"How can I get the best one for the cheapest price?"—becomes in effect a socially accepted license to *steal* information. If step one of the buyer's system is to *give* as little information as possible, step two is to *take* as much information from the salesperson as he is willing to give, which traditionally is *everything* in a stage-two market—his time, his expertise, and indirectly, his money.

Time: In addition to the obvious time that salespeople give to buyers while presenting in face-to-face meetings, there is also: preparation time; driving time; time developing RFP's (requests for proposals), quotes, bids, and designs; not to mention the unlimited follow-up time that customers automatically expect.

Expertise: Buyers ask for professional advice, layouts, designs, and information of all sorts, and salespeople willingly respond. Office furniture salespeople, landscapers, engineers, advertising layout specialists, and so on, create elaborate designs, only to have their expert ideas pirated without permission or penalty.

Money: Salespeople incur out-of-pocket expenses which indirectly increase the cost of the sale—travel expenses, entertainment, meals, gifts, and the like. But also, since *time is money*, all of the time given by salespeople to customers is money given, as well.

What the buyer really wants is a free education from the salesperson, but without any obligation in return. In effect, the buyer tempts the salesperson by hanging a carrot out that suggests, "If you hope to make the sale, show me whatcha got," thereby baiting the seller to give away his valuable information. Sometimes the buyer has no intention of changing vendors, but instead he actually uses the "stolen" information to beat down his existing supplier to get the lowest possible price.

Step Three

Having given little information to the salesperson but having received much information in return, the next step in the buyer's process is to stall for time. He accomplishes this with a remark like "I need time to think it over," followed by some version of "I'll get back to you," "I'll give you a call," or "I'll be in touch."

There are three reasons why the buyer stalls for time at this juncture. Either he wants to retain the salesperson as an unpaid consultant because he may need more information; or, he may find after shopping around that this particular salesperson has the best deal, and therefore doesn't want to alienate him too early in the process; or, the buyer is finished with the salesperson, but doesn't want to hurt his feelings by saying "no." In this last case, he is simply being polite, in spite of the fact that he may have no intention of keeping his word. These white lies among others have become a socially acceptable phenomenon in the buyer/seller relationship.

Buyers are well-armed with an arsenal of creative expressions which they use to disguise their true intentions:

- "I need to sleep on it."

- "I might be interested."
- "Maybe I'll buy one soon."
- "I want to discuss it with so-and-so."
- "I'll have to take this to my boss for his approval."
- "This will have to be presented to a committee."
- "I never buy anything the first time that I see it."
- "Your product looks good. If I ever have a need for it, I'll let you know."
- "Whether we do this or not depends on upcoming budget decisions."
- "I'm not ready to buy yet, but I'm sure I will be in the near future."
- "I'm getting three bids before I make a decision."
- "I want to shop around."
- "I need to think it over."

Every salesperson can relate with these types of empty promises, and knows the frustration of working with customers who use them.

Step Four

Once the buyer has compared features, benefits, and prices and has finished "shopping around," occasionally he does keep his word and actually makes a purchase from one of the salespeople to whom he made a promise. More often, however, he doesn't need the salesperson any longer and is ready to dump him.

In this latter case, the next step for the buyer is to *not do what he said he would do*, namely get back to the salesperson. This inaction on the buyer's part is meant to convey the message to the seller that he is not interested, that his answer is "no," and that he wants the salesperson to leave him alone—basically a don't-call-me-I'll-call-you message.

The Buyer's Process Summarized

In brief and concise form, the universal buyer's process is:

> Step 1: **Show interest**, but hold onto your cards by sharing as little information as possible; even **lie if necessary**.
>
> Step 2: Beg, borrow, and **steal** as much **information** as possible while giving up as little as possible in return.
>
> Step 3: **Stall for time** to shop around and steal more information from other competing salespeople.
>
> Step 4: **Don't get back** to any of the salespeople involved except to the one from whom you finally buy.

Again, this four-step system—used instinctively in whole or in part by *all* buyers—is designed to control the buyer/seller tug of war for the purpose of allaying the buyer's fears. It is innate, well-practiced, highly effective, reliable, and extremely powerful. It has withstood the test of time, and works unusually well to protect the buyer's interests. This has infuriated and humiliated salespeople for years because it forces them into the "follower," or inferior, position. Many talented people have been driven from the field for lack of knowing how to *take the lead* and overcome the subtle yet powerful tactics embedded in the buyer's system.

7

Sellers *Show* Their Cards

Commissioned salespeople—and let's be clear, even *salaried* salespeople are commissioned in that if they don't produce, they're sooner or later fired—depend on buyers for their livelihood. Naturally, then, the seller doesn't want to "bite the hand that feeds him," so he instinctively yields to the buyer's wishes and demands. If the buyer says, "show me your cards," the seller willingly follows and eagerly cooperates, hoping that he holds a card or two that the buyer will purchase.

This "show-all" and "tell-all" mentality on the part of the salesperson is at the center of what we refer to as the "traditional seller's system." The system is an aggregate of selling strategies that have grown out of the stages of a product's life cycle in response to the needs of the buyer. While we discussed in Chapter 4 the strategies of how to sell in each of those stages, it is remarkable how those same strategies dovetail to form a complete selling system. By way of quick review, then:

Step One

The first step in the seller's system is to "bring it to their attention" or create a need in the hope of finding buyer interest. The focus is on marketing campaigns and prospecting strategies, ranging from infomercials to cold calls. Step one might be compared to the first step in the sport of fishing. Experienced catfish anglers will know that it is common practice to place liver in a burlap bag and throw it in the water to attract the fish. Similarly, the seller tries to "attract" his prospects.

Step Two

Once the salesperson finds some indication of interest from a prospective buyer, his second step is to present product information in the form of features and benefits, a stage-two phenomenon in a product's life cycle. The whole idea is to educate the buyer by "showing his cards" in the hope of convincing him that "This is the best product." In comparison to fishing, this is equivalent to the angler using his most attractive lures and tastiest baits to entice the fish to bite.

Step two is, in effect, a "presentation" step. It requires a "persuasion mentality" from the salesperson, where his goal is to convince the buyer to purchase from him. *Pure* stage-two selling is to give 100 percent of the "dog and pony show" 100 percent of the time. It is important to not prejudge the buyer, which might lead to the salesperson giving abbreviated or haphazard presentations. Based on the belief that "showing" and "telling" are the keys to making the sale, exorbitant amounts of time and money have been, and continue to be, "invested" on training salespeople to become expert presenters. In practice, presenting features and benefits has been, and still is, the modus operandi for most salespeople today.

Step Three

Remember, the buyer's fear of being taken advantage of causes him to be wary of the salesperson immediately. On top of his innate distrust, the buyer also resists any and all persuasive tactics used by the salesperson. The result is that he stalls and raises objections. Like the fish resists when it is initially hooked, so does the prospect resist.

The seller's job, therefore, has been to attempt to overcome the buyer's resistance. Typically this involves the use of trial-closing strategies, coupled with the art of negotiating his way through the buyer's objections, and eventually settling on a price that is agreeable to both parties (stage three in a product's life cycle). The problem is that many prospects fight like whales, while anglers fishing for catfish are unsuspecting and ill-equipped; hence the majority get away.

Step Four

If the seller was fortunate in step three, he made the sale; more likely, he did not. In either case, the next step in the seller's system is to "follow up" with the customer. With a prospect who actually buys, this follow-up is more commonly called customer service.

All other follow-up involves "chasing" the prospect in the hope of catching him, which is as futile as trying to catch the fish that got away. This "hope factor" is an important one to understand. The buyer's broken promise is meant to send a clear message to the seller to leave him alone. However, most sellers would much rather pursue a known contact than to start all over by having to find a complete stranger. A glimmer of hope *feels* better than no hope at all. The traditional selling process teaches the salesperson that a "maybe someday" is better than getting a definite and final "no."

The Seller's System Summarized

Like the buyer's system, the seller's system is a four-step process:

Step 1: **Find interest** through various marketing and prospecting strategies.

Step 2: **Give a presentation** by showing all of your cards in the hope that your cards are better than the other guy's.

Step 3: **Overcome stalls and objections,** negotiate price, and attempt to close the sale by coming to a mutual agreement.

Step 4: **Service** them when they buy; **chase** them if they don't buy.

It's a Vicious Circle

Anyone who has ever sold for a living can relate to the endless circularity of having to suffer through these same steps over and over again in their efforts to make a sale. Salespeople try to cope with their monotonous, time-wasting, and often degrading routine by voicing such light-hearted sayings as "If you throw enough mud against the wall, some of it is bound to stick," and "You've got to kiss a lot of frogs before you find your prince."

Where levity of this type has its place in helping people cope with such frustrating situations, the traditional seller's life is no laughing matter. The "treatment" that salespeople as a group have taken from buyers day after day for years is actually "mistreatment," bordering in many cases on emotional abuse. Such abuse can only exist because of the imbalance of power that has been perpetuated in the relationship between the buyer and the seller.

8

Playing a New Game

If you don't *lead* with a plan of your own, you are automatically *following* somebody else's plan.

While most salespeople might argue that they do have some type of plan when they sell, the truth is that their plan often naively follows a fractured version of the golden rule—*he who has the gold makes the rules*. Since buyers "have the gold," so to speak, they make the rules that count in the final analysis. In actuality, the seller's plan is to follow the plan of the buyer, since he is the one with the money.

The fact is that salespeople are *totally* dependent on buyers for their income. This is not true in the reverse—buyers do *not* depend on sellers for their livelihood, which automatically tips the balance of power in the buyer's favor.

Figure 4

To add insult to injury, salespeople have been conditioned to behave as if "the customer is *always* right." The trouble is, this implies that salespeople have *no* rights, which is exactly how the majority of salespeople feel most of the time.

Comparing the Two Systems Side By Side

The following chart is a helpful reference to better understand this imbalance of power:

Buyer's Process	**Seller's Process**
1. Show interest, withhold information, lie if necessary	1. Find interest
2. Steal information	2. Present features and benefits
3. Stall, promise to get back	3. Overcome stalls and objections
4. Don't get back	4. Chase

The Battle Is Over Before It Begins

When you read the above chart from right to left rather than left to right, the imbalance of power becomes very obvious.

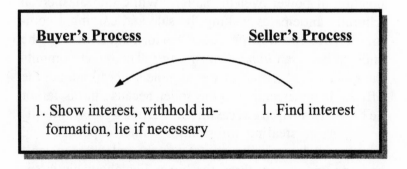

Buyer's Process	**Seller's Process**
1. Show interest, withhold information, lie if necessary	1. Find interest

It takes very little expression of interest from the buyer to raise the hopes of the seller to the point of believing that he has a "live one." Typically, the seller gets visibly excited whenever he finds an interested party. The buyer senses this, and knows that he can misrepresent his degree of interest in order to manipulate the salesperson into openly giving away his valuable information, time, and expertise. The truth is that the seller is completely at the mercy of, and is *reactive* to, the apparent interest of the buyer, whether real or feigned.

The problem gets even worse in step two in that this is where the actual theft occurs.

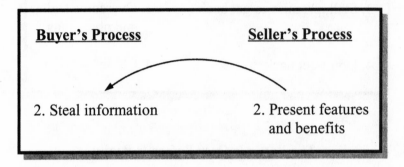

Buyer's Process   **Seller's Process**

2. Steal information   2. Present features
                          and benefits

While salespeople labor passionately at their "dog and pony shows," buyers pilfer the valuable information under the guise of interest, taking full advantage of their position of power over the seller. While the salesperson naturally anticipates making the sale and earning a commission for his well-practiced performance, in truth he ends up being an *unpaid consultant!* The buyer commits the sanctioned "crime" of stealing the seller blind, but the offense is undetectable to the seller because in his fervor he becomes a willing *accessory* to a crime against himself!

As if stealing information, time, expertise, and money—at least indirectly—from the salesperson isn't bad enough, in step three the buyer lies about his intentions.

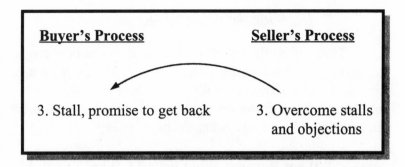

The buyer stalls for several possible reasons. First, he might need additional information, and therefore has to keep the seller *hoping* that he will buy in order to access that information. Second, the buyer may be politely trying to get rid of the seller, but doesn't want to create hurt feelings by rejecting him with a blatant "no." Third, in a few cases he will eventually need the salesperson in order to buy the product.

Step four is the straw that finally breaks the salesperson's back, namely, the flagrant avoidance of the seller by the buyer who promised to get back, and didn't.

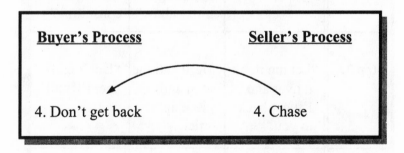

All salespeople know that the vast majority of time the buyer does *not* get back, even though he promised that he would. Believing that the buyer meant what he said, the seller then chases the buyer in his futile attempt to close the deal.

Decoding the Buyer's Language

More often than not, the gulf that exists between the buyer's system and the seller's system results from a breakdown in communication. The actual breakdown is imbedded in the differences between what the buyer said, what the seller heard, and what the buyer meant.

Buyer's System	What Buyer Said	What Seller Heard	What Buyer Meant
Step 1.	"I'm interested in hearing what you have to offer."	"I've got a 'live' one!"	"I'm shopping around and comparing prices."
Step 2.	"Tell me all about it."	"He's ready for me to convince him to buy."	"I want free information and unpaid consulting."
Step 3.	"Let me think it over and I'll get back to you."	"He'll call me soon and place an order."	"Don't call me, I'll call you."
Step 4.	(Does not get back as promised.)	"He either forgot or he's very busy, so I'll follow up."	"No, it's over!"

So Who's Really in Control Here?

Is there any doubt? The traditional seller's process is *totally reactive* to the buyer's process. The buyer leads and the seller follows; the buyer says "jump" and the seller asks "how high?"; the buyer dictates and the seller obeys.

The truth is that buyers have been leading salespeople around by the proverbial nose since time immemorial. However, it isn't the seller's fault that such abuse has persisted, considering that:

- sales managers and VP's of sales have instructed their salespeople to "present, present, and present some more" as their core selling philosophy.

- the buyer's system is both cunning and relentless, and it is saturated with subtle nuances designed to maneuver the seller into the subservient or inferior position.

- "hope springs eternal in the human heart," especially in salespeople, who tend by nature to be very optimistic and believing of the customer.

- nobody likes rejection, especially salespeople who face it daily, so they will do anything possible to avoid hearing the buyer say "no," including going along with the buyer's charades.

- salespeople have long felt frustrated and degraded by the imbalance of power in the buyer/seller relationship, but they have been instructed to accept it as "part of the territory" of their job responsibilities.

Let's Give Credit Where Credit Is Due

Given these obstacles, salespeople haven't just lain down and played dead. To their credit, they have tried to defend themselves and fight back to capture the lead and to gain control of the selling interaction.

In step one, for example, they've worked to get better at prospecting and marketing. The problem is that buyers soon catch on and thereafter get better at withholding information and lying. In step two, salespeople work hard at giving better presentations, but as we've said, this just gives buyers more information to steal. In step three, salespeople learn new techniques to overcome objections and close the deal, but this causes the buyer to get more creative at stalling for time. And in step four, sellers work harder at managing their time and becoming better organized so as not to lose prospects "through the cracks." However, buyers get better at blocking the salesperson's attempts to communicate by installing automated phone systems and by training their phone personnel to "guard the gate" against all unwelcomed calls.

But the Attempts Have Been Futile

The point is that the seller's attempts to gain control of the buyer/seller interaction haven't worked in the long run. As with certain diseases, the stronger the medicine we use to fight it, the more resistant the disease becomes. We once thought that we had tuberculosis beaten with our powerful antibiotics, yet today the disease is on the rise. The antibiotics that once worked are now not strong enough to combat the new strains of the disease.

By comparison, the harder that salespeople work to gain control through traditional selling strategies, the stronger and more resilient the buyer's system becomes. It has been an endless struggle, with the salesperson never really gaining the upper hand.

This Imbalance of Power in the Buyer/Seller Relationship Must Change

There are many reasons why this imbalance of power must be corrected. First, for the sake of human dignity, no one deserves to be emotionally used and abused, salespeople included.

Second, sales has been loosely referred to as a "profession," but few would agree that it has achieved the status of a *true* profession. Consider the field of medicine: Would a doctor, who incidentally must also "sell" his services, waste valuable time giving away free advice hoping to persuade the patient to "buy" from him? How ludicrous! Yet this is exactly what salespeople do all day, everyday—buyers holding their cards, sellers showing their cards—all in the name of doing business and making a living.

Third, when people refuse to be taken advantage of by others, they naturally feel better about themselves. As a result, their self-worth improves, and consequently, so does their performance. Obviously, this would pertain to salespeople, as well.

Survival In Sales Today Demands Correcting This Imbalance

As important as these reasons might have been for salespeople to play a different game by learning a whole new set of rules, there has been no *urgent* reason for them to change until now. With the arrival of warp-speed change, however, there *is* an urgent reason—namely, those who *don't* change aren't likely to survive for long.

Business is now changing faster than the mind can comprehend. The name of the game from this point forth is *efficiency,* and the traditional selling system is anything but efficient! This is because it is fraught with time-wasters created by the buyer that impede the selling process.

Make no mistake about it, the buyer's system is *extremely* efficient *for the buyer.* But the traditional seller's system is appallingly *inefficient* for the seller because it is **reactive** to the time-consuming strategies built into the buyer's process. Once a salesperson falls prey to the clutches of the buyer's system, he wastes **untold** sums of time, *even though time is his most valuable asset!*

Leadership Selling: The New Challenge

Salespeople must make it their number one priority to become leaders in their selling efforts. By leading rather than following, they automatically increase their efficiency, which in turn increases their earnings.

The way this is accomplished is through Leadership Selling. *It consists of taking control and methodically moving the customer's attention back to his true buying motive, again, to his initial problem.* This approach vastly reduces the opportunity for buyers to waste the salesperson's time with an "I'm just shopping around" attitude. By skillfully diverting the customer's attention away from price and toward his problem, the salesperson expedites his opportunity to sell a "solution." And once price is no longer the primary issue, he is thereby able to realize a greater profit.

It is important to remember, however, that buyers will resist your attempts to move their attention from price to problems. As much as consumers appreciate the professional service that you are performing *after* you have engaged them in the process of identifying their problem, in the beginning they are much more comfortable trying to stay focused on price.

It is therefore mandatory that the salesperson take *full* control of the selling interaction, but not by any of the traditional methods that one normally associates with "taking control"—dominating the conversation, using high-pressure tactics, and the like. In fact, the salesperson's control must be so skillfully implemented that the customer will *feel* completely in control, even though the seller will be controlling the interaction at every turn.

Such skills represent a radical departure from those which most salespeople are accustomed to using. They require learning a *totally* new selling methodology—that is, adopting a *leadership* mentality that is critical to master if one expects to excel in the field of sales today, and beyond.

Part III

The Pre-Game Preparation

Successful athletes must prepare in specific ways in advance of the actual game in order to perform optimally when game time arrives—weight training, proper nutrition, and the like. PART III addresses the important factors that prepare the salesperson to become proficient at Leadership Selling. THE PRE-GAME PREPARATION is as essential to the mastery of Leadership Selling as a strong foundation is to the structural integrity of a towering building.

9

I'm OK

Just as a master gardener knows that he must prepare his soil well if he is to produce prize-winning vegetables, so must a Leadership Salesperson understand that he, too, must prepare properly in order to reap a bountiful harvest. For this reason, it is necessary to assess yourself in the following four areas before implementing the actual techniques of Leadership Selling:

- your self-esteem (Chapter 9)
- your understanding of how to stay focused (Chapter 10)
- your ability to implement a plan of action (Chapter 11)
- your attitude (Chapter 12)

One of the preparatory questions that we ask a salesperson who wants to master Leadership Selling is, "How would you rate your own level of self-esteem?" This is because there is a direct correlation between how a person values himself and his sales performance. Low self-esteem tends to manifest itself in negative ways, such as not doing the required selling behaviors, lack of motivation, pessimism, lack of self-discipline, and fear of adopting new techniques that lie outside one's comfort zone.

The truth is that salespeople can only perform to a level that is equal to their belief in their own self-worth. This concept is not new or revolutionary; it is evident in the world around us that people who feel good about themselves generally function better in life than those who do not. They tend to achieve more, earn more, are healthier and happier, and so on. For these reasons alone it is important that *all* people work to achieve and maintain high levels of self-esteem. But it is *especially* important for salespeople to do so.

The challenge in Leadership Selling is to *take control of the sales call*. Buyers never willingly surrender the control that they are used to having. They will resist you, so you cannot go ill-equipped into battle with a balsawood sword. Your coat of armor will be your self-esteem, and the stronger it is, the better protected you will be as you lead them through their own resistance.

The Relationship Between Self and Behavior

There is a direct correlation between one's feelings about "self" and one's behavior or level of performance. Imagine a vertical scale from 0-10, where the left side of the scale represents one's feelings about himself and the right side represents his actual behavior.

SELF   **BEHAVIOR**

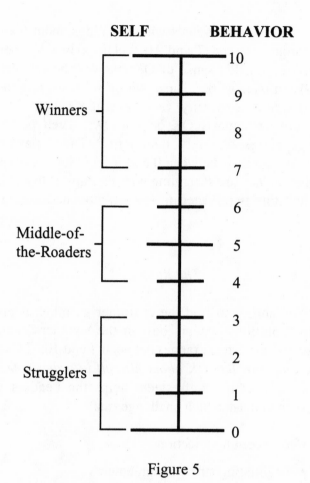

Figure 5

Again, one will only perform to a level that is consistent with how he feels about him-SELF. As this relates specifically to selling, a salesperson's behavior will be, on the average, not more than one above or one below his level of self-esteem. For example, if a salesperson's self-esteem is 5, his job performance will range between 4 and 6.

Note the three subdivisions of the scale on the left margin: winners (7-10), middle-of-the-roaders (4-6), and strugglers (0-3). Individuals whose feelings about themselves range between 7 and 10 feel largely OK about themselves, and this sense of OKness will be reflected positively in their work. Those whose self-esteem is between 4 and 6 generally feel "average" about their worth—not particularly OK or Not OK. Their performance is correspondingly mediocre. Those persons whose self-esteem is between 0 and 3 feel Not OK about themselves. They are struggling with feelings of low self-worth, and this is reflected in less effectiveness in their jobs.

The Rule

The ability to find the customer's problems and sell him "solutions" occurs best in the "winners" zone where one's self-esteem ranges between 7 and 10. This is because *one must feel OK about himself in order to lead the sales call.* High self-esteem helps the Leadership Salesperson to master such challenges as:

- overcoming rejection

- negotiating stronger agreements

- asking the tough questions

- persisting when necessary

- refusing to submit to the buyer's rules

One can count on the fact that the buyer will not roll over and play dead when the salesperson attempts to change the rules on him. At first he will resist, and his resistance can be both frustrating and discouraging until the seller becomes proficient at the required skills. Since perfecting Leadership Selling techniques takes practice, it is important to give time and attention to the matter of developing and maintaining a high level of self-esteem.

It is not uncommon for us to receive calls from CEOs who request that we train their salespeople to become better negotiators. In response to this question, we usually ask, "How tough are your people?" meaning "How high is their self-esteem?" We ask this because self-esteem is a prerequisite to being a strong negotiator, and it is fruitless to work on negotiating skills until self-esteem is properly addressed.

How Can One Assess His Level of Self-Esteem?

Determining where one's self-esteem ranks on the previous graph takes some introspection. As a point of reference, it is commonly agreed that approximately 20 percent of the people in the general population are in the 7-10 range, 60 percent are in the 4-6 range, and 20 percent are in the 0-3 range. This is why it is so important to confront the issue of self-esteem in oneself before tackling this new selling approach: on the average, only 20 percent of salespeople will have self-esteem that is naturally high enough to function in the 7-10 range. All others are advised to purposefully work to raise it to a higher level.

There are three convenient ways to measure self-esteem. First, ask yourself the question, "On the average, how do I feel about myself *independent of* the various roles that I play in life?" "On the average" is important, because everyone has times when they feel better or worse about themselves.

A second way is to rank your sales performance, and then—since performance reflects feelings about oneself—infer what that means about your current level of self-esteem.

Third, because "birds of a feather flock together," a person can observe his friends and close associates for some clue as to his own feelings of self-worth. It's only natural that people tend to associate with others whose self-esteem reflects their own.

More important, though, than determining one's feelings about "self" at any given moment is to make sure that one is working to improve them. You may have heard the expression "Where a person is in life isn't as important as the direction in which he is going." The truth of this saying applies directly to self-esteem, which is not a fixed entity. It is in constant flux and can definitely be raised, given the right effort. The good news is that as it improves, so will one's sales performance improve accordingly.

How Does One Build and Maintain High Levels of Self-Esteem?

#1

Start by understanding the nature of your *true* self-worth, beyond how you *feel* about yourself at any given moment in time. You are, always have been, and always will be a 10. Feelings about yourself can fluctuate depending on what's happening in your life at any given time. Yet the knowledge that you are worth a 10 will help you maintain better feelings about yourself, *regardless* of your failures and the normal ups and downs that are a part of life.

We cannot emphasize this point enough. *The biggest problem that arises with making permanent behavior change in people is the belief deep down that they don't deserve success when it comes!* This is why so many people achieve high levels of success in sales initially, only to backslide to a state of mediocrity. Unknowingly, they have stepped outside of their comfort zone in terms of their belief about their own self-worth, and they soon return to it so that they don't remain uncomfortable too long.

#2

Remind yourself on a regular basis that you *are* a 10. Daily self-affirmations help, as do signs located in strategic places that you see regularly—such as on your bathroom mirror at home or at your work station—that say, "I'm a 10!"

#3

Make sure that you deliberately associate with people who perceive you as a 10 and are willing to tell you so. We have been misled for so long that our worth is solely a function of our behavior that we need to be periodically reminded that we're OK *regardless* of the failures that we experience occasionally on the job.

#4

Become an expert or a specialist at something that interests you. As you gradually become proficient, your self-confidence will grow, and correspondingly your feelings about yourself will improve.

#5

Know that it's OK to fail. When your feelings of self-esteem are rooted in your behavior, it feels like you can't risk failure because failing would mean that something is the matter with your "self." But the truth is, **"you" can never be a failure.** You are always a 10, although you can certainly *do* something that fails.

Ironically, what helps build self-esteem faster than anything else is to risk failing. There are only two possible outcomes—either you will fail or you will succeed. Yet both are beneficial. If you fail, that's OK! With the support of those who see you as a 10, you'll learn a valuable lesson that will help you succeed the next time. If you succeed, your self-confidence grows, and therefore so does the opportunity to raise your self-esteem.

#6

Take time to make a list of all of your previous successes, those things that you have done well. You may be surprised that the list is longer than you might have initially predicted. Take credit for those successes; you deserve it! Give yourself some recognition by patting yourself on the back for " jobs well done!"

#7

Every time you feel that you have failed in some way, review the situation and determine the lesson that you learned from the experience. Lessons learned turn negatives into positives. This eliminates the negative impact of the experience on your self-esteem. We do not start out in life as a zero in self-worth and then fight our way up the ladder. To the contrary, we start out as 10s, and the negative influences that we experience in life tend to adversely affect our feelings about ourselves.

When we learn to manage those negatives, we also learn to maintain positive self-esteem. The best way to do this is to turn the negatives into positives. That's what a lesson learned accomplishes. And you can best turn a lesson learned into a positive if you project how you're going to benefit from that lesson.

#8

There are many good books written on the subject of improving self-concept and raising self-esteem. Since people generally achieve whatever they focus on, we encourage you to make it a part of your professional routine to actively review such resources.

#9

If there is a negative influence in your life that is adversely affecting your feelings of self-worth, *you must resolve that situation* as soon as possible. ***Nothing destroys self-esteem faster than constant negativity in your life.*** Whether that negative influence is a person, a certain environment, or a set of circumstances, you must look squarely at the problem and design a plan to remedy it, or your self-esteem will almost certainly not improve.

The Point

As valuable as these guidelines are, our purpose in this chapter has not been to write an exhaustive list of methods that you can use to improve self-esteem. Hopefully, one or more of these suggestions will be helpful. If you'd like additional information, there are many other resources available for raising self-esteem. Often it only takes changing one or two behaviors to make a significant difference. *Our primary intention here is to emphasize how important it is that you maintain your feelings of self-worth so that you can readily assume the leadership role in your relationship with customers.*

The bottom line is that the days of salespeople acting as slaves to the buyer must end. Salespeople who work at maintaining high levels of self-esteem will be the best prepared to take on the challenge of Leadership Selling, and by so doing, to reverse the inequities built into traditional selling strategies.

At first you can expect the buyer to resist your efforts to gain control. Sometimes the demonstration of his resistance will be open and obvious, sometimes it will be more subtle and hidden. But there will be resistance nonetheless, often in the form of price concerns. Yet salespeople who properly develop their feelings of self-worth will be prepared to lead the customer through that resistance rather than succumb to it.

10

Staying Focused

Very few people would disagree with the notions that—

- what one focuses on is what one gets,

  and

- if one is consistent in his behavior, one will be consistent in achieving results.

Yet two of the primary reasons that salespeople fail to achieve their goals are the loss of focus and inconsistent behavior. Goal-setting is an effective strategy to help keep one's attention focused and one's activity consistent.

~

Quite possibly no subject has been written about in business more than the "importance of" and the "how to's" of goal-setting. It is only common sense that if a person knows *where* he is going that he is much more likely to get there! Many people claim to have goals of one sort or another, but many of those goals are vague and poorly defined, and are therefore difficult if not impossible to achieve. As an example, just consider how short-lived most New Year's resolutions are. The trouble is, merely setting goals doesn't mean that one will necessarily achieve them.

Since there are many resources out there on the subjects of goal-setting and goal-achievement, it is not our intention to fill this chapter with suggestions that have been made many times in many places by many experts. Nevertheless, there are two key elements that are important to understand before proceeding with the subject of Leadership Selling: (1) knowing how to set *achievable* goals, and (2) developing the motivation, or sense of urgency, to actually achieve them.

Setting Achievable Goals

Perhaps you're already familiar with the concept that in order to achieve one's goals, the goals must be SMART, which is an acronym for:

Specific

Measurable

Attainable

Realistic

Time-framed

We agree that this is a good recipe for goal-setting; however, we feel that there are some essential ingredients missing. Therefore, let's review the meaning of SMART goals, followed by a discussion of the ABC's of how to put your SMART goals to work.

SMART Goals

Suppose that one has the goal to flap his arms as fast as he can and raise his body off the ground until his head touches the ceiling, all within five minutes. To ascertain whether or not this goal is achievable, he must ask himself, "Is this a SMART goal?"

- First, is it *Specific*? Specificity is determined by whether or not one would know exactly *what* to do in order to achieve the stated goal. In this case the goal is very specific—flap your arms as fast as you can, etc.

- Second, is it *Measurable*? Is there a way to determine whether or not one is achieving, or has achieved, his goal? Here one would only need a yardstick or tape measure with which to establish a starting and ending height—so yes, the goal in question is measurable.

- Third, is the goal *Attainable*? Can it be done? To the best of our knowledge this particular phenomenon has never been accomplished; and from everything we know about physics and aerodynamics, the goal appears to be unattainable.

- Fourth, is it *Realistic*? A goal is realistic if it is attainable within the time-frame specified. In this case, the goal to flap one's arms and raise oneself to the ceiling isn't realistic because it is not achievable within *any* time frame, least of all within five minutes. Another goal, on the other hand, might be quite attainable but not so within the time-frame allowed. For example, a person may have the goal to run one mile in ten seconds. While running a mile *is* achievable, it can *not* be done in ten seconds. Such a goal, then, would be unrealistic.

- Fifth, is the goal *Time-framed*? That is, is its accomplishment set within certain time parameters? In this example, clearly it is—*within five minutes.*

Now let's recall the question: Is the goal "to flap one's arms as fast as possible and raise one's body off the ground until one's head touches the ceiling within five minutes" a SMART goal? The answer is absolutely not, since only three of the five conditions have been met.

> *In order for a goal to be a SMART goal, all five of the conditions must be met.*

If one or more of the conditions is not satisfied, then the goal will not be realized no matter how determined one is to achieve it.

The ABC's of SMART Goal-Setting

Our experience is that many salespeople who have in fact set SMART goals *still* don't achieve them. How is this possible? The answer is that the ABC's of SMART goal-setting have been overlooked, namely that goals must also be:

> **A**ccountable
>
> **B**ehavior-based
>
> **C**ontrollable

- **Accountable:** It is extremely rare for a person to possess the self-discipline sufficient to be truly accountable to himself as it concerns achieving his own goals. Most people need the help of an authority outside of themselves, which is much more normal. All human beings are creatures of habit, and therefore tend to adopt unique patterns of behavior. Collectively, these patterns comprise one's "comfort zone." The natural tendency is to resist changing any behaviors that extend beyond the boundaries of one's comfort zone. You *must* be held accountable to someone outside of yourself if you are serious about reaching your SMART goals.

  This tendency to habituate one's behavior is why it's so important that you arrange to be held accountable for your goals to someone other than yourself. If you are part of a sales force, the natural person for the job is your sales manager or your vice president of sales. Go to that person and discuss the importance of being held accountable for your goals and the changes that you want to make. If this is not possible because you are independently employed, consider forming a small group of associates who would meet regularly to monitor each member's progress. The bottom line is that you must be held accountable to someone outside of yourself if you are serious about reaching your SMART goals.

- **Behavior-based:** Many people when they set a goal focus on the end result rather than on the means by which to achieve it—that is, on their behavior. Let's take Marie, for example, who works as a real estate agent. She has set a goal to sell one million dollars of real estate in a year. The truth is that Marie has little control over who will eventually buy, how much they will pay, or when it will happen. But she does have *total* control over her own behavior, and this is where she should concentrate her efforts.

   Although Marie followed the guidelines to the letter of setting a SMART goal, nevertheless, her emphasis was on the *result* rather than on the *means* by which to attain it, and was therefore not a *behavior-based* goal. Instead, her goal should target the appropriate behaviors that are required to sell one million dollars worth of property within a year's time.

   The trouble is that the definition of such behaviors is often limited to surface activities—making, let's say, forty face-to-face appointments per month, ten per week, two per day, and so on.

   The broader definition of "behavior-based," which is the one we have in mind, is not confined to *quantitative* matters, but includes *qualitative* factors, as well. That is, the term "behavior-based" relates not only to *what* activities one does, but also to *how* he performs them. In Marie's two face-to-face appointments per day, for example, she might well concentrate on specific Leadership Selling techniques with certain customers, taking into consideration their unique buying styles.

• **Controllable:** One can only achieve goals that he can control, and all anyone can control ultimately is their own behavior. This is why we emphasize how critical it is that one's goals must be based on his behavior. As we said, SMART goals are necessary but not sufficient by themselves. How can one know if his goal is Attainable and Realistic if he doesn't have control over them?

The Relationship Between Goal Achievement and Motivation

Randy is a heavy smoker. He is thirty-seven years old, does strenuous physical labor as a construction worker, eats nutritiously, and generally is in good health. When he visits the doctor for his annual physical checkup, he receives a clean bill of health. The doctor does recommend, however, that he stop smoking; and since Randy has noticed some shortness of breath, he agrees with the doctor and makes it his goal to stop. He tries to quit, and after a period of time finds himself becoming easily irritated, and eventually gives up the goal altogether of breaking his smoking habit.

George, a car salesman, is also thirty-seven years old and, like Randy, is a smoker. One day he is suddenly stricken with chest pains, collapses, and is rushed to the emergency room of the hospital. The next day he undergoes quadruple by-pass heart surgery, and days later the doctor tells George that if he doesn't stop smoking he'll die prematurely. George makes it his immediate goal to quit smoking, throws away his cigarettes, and never smokes again in spite of the fact that he is tempted on several occasions to resume his old habit.

What is the difference between Randy's situation and George's? One thing—*motivation*, and nothing more. George's situation is urgent and life-threatening, whereas Randy does not believe that his situation is urgent, and reacts accordingly. It's that simple.

What Does Motivation Have to Do with Selling?

Salespeople must understand that setting achievable goals and staying focused on those goals to completion *is urgent*. In fact, it is *very* urgent. The market situation that salespeople find themselves in today is far more like George's scenario than Randy's. Technological advancement, along with the information explosion that it has ignited, has caused such a rapid rate of change in the business world today that changing the way we sell *is* urgent if one expects to thrive in the profession.

Leadership Selling is not just a new methodology for salespeople who are bored and simply want to "try something different." It is a revolutionary shift in the way that salespeople work, and it is intended for the "Georges" in the profession, not the "Randys." It requires a high degree of motivation because it involves changing one's behaviors. And behaviors can really only be changed significantly when one stays *focused* on change through the ABCs of SMART goal-setting.

11

Developing a Game Plan

Just as reading a book on golf doesn't by itself make one a skilled golfer, a salesperson is not likely to become proficient at Leadership Selling merely by reading this book. Reading is important for acquiring new knowledge, and possibly even in changing one's attitude. But gaining new knowledge and adopting a different attitude don't automatically change one's sales behavior; they simply precede it. Actual behavior change is the result of *applying* one's knowledge, which is more difficult to do than acquiring it, and requires more time. In fact, the more individuals who are involved, the more time it takes, as demonstrated in the following chart.

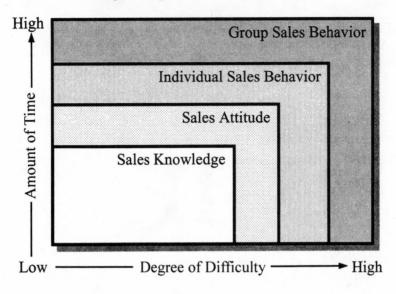

Figure 6

The truth is that in order to perfect this new selling approach, it may be necessary for the reader to change several behaviors that have become habits over the years. At first this might seem difficult, but only because it involves learning new skills. With a strong commitment and clear focus, Leadership Selling can indeed be mastered. A well-defined plan of action is extremely important in this regard, hence the purpose of this chapter is to help you develop such a plan.

Step 1: Be Accountable to Someone

We said earlier in our discussion of the ABC's of goal-setting that it is important to be accountable to someone other than yourself. The same is true with your plan of action. Assuming that you are answering to the same person, together you must agree on regular meetings that will serve as checkpoints to ensure that your progress will be monitored.

Step 2: You Get What You Measure

If you want to change a behavior, measuring that change will help to keep you focused and achieve your goal more quickly. It is too early at this point to define exactly which behaviors you will want to change until they are more clearly defined in Part IV. Whichever ones you decide to work on changing, it will be necessary to measure your starting point in terms of that particular behavior.

For example, let's suppose that you want to change behavior X. First establish a base line by charting how many times behavior X occurs over a specified period of time, say, one week. Don't attempt to *interpret* the data; simply record it. This establishes the initial benchmark against which all future progress will be measured.

Periodically thereafter until the particular behavior is thoroughly ingrained—that is, until you "own" it as opposed to just "knowing" it—measure your progress on the targeted behavior. If it isn't changing as fast as you had predicted, adjust your plan to expedite your progress. Obviously, the person to whom you are being held accountable must play an instrumental role in the measuring process.

Step 3: Keep a Daily Behavior Journal

One always behaves in ways that are consistent

with his predominant thoughts. An excellent technique for staying focused on the importance of continually developing Leadership Selling behaviors is to keep a daily journal of selling activities.

There are many ways to design a journal, but above all, the format should be congruent with your own record-keeping preferences. The common mistake that people make when they first begin learning this new selling system is attempting to change too many behaviors at once. The easier and more effective way to change one's behaviors is to designate one specific behavior to be changed at a time. Chart the progress of this particular behavior until you are doing it consistently before moving on to the next behavior to be changed.

An easy way to chart the progress of your behavioral change is to set up a form to be filled out after each and every sales call. It should take *no more* than sixty seconds to complete the form, otherwise it becomes too time-consuming and the tendency is to postpone it and soon forget to fill it out altogether.

Again, design a format that works for you. Some people prefer to incorporate the journal into their daily planners; others keep a separate notebook that they use solely for journaling purposes; still others track the information on their personal computers. Whichever format you select, we strongly suggest that you include at a minimum the information that appears in Figure 7.

__Daily Behavior Journal__

Date:_____

Name of Contact:_____

Company Called On: _____

Targeted Behavior: _____

Circle One of the Following (0 = did not attempt; 10 = performed to perfection):

   0 1 2 3 4 5 6 7 8 9 10

Lesson Learned: _____
_____
_____
_____
_____
_____

Figure 7

Step 4: Practice, Practice, and Practice Some More

The world of athletics furnishes an excellent model for how to actuate changes in behavior. In every sport at every level, athletes perfect their skills through the "Three-R's" of behavioral learning: **R**eview, **R**einforcement, and **R**epetition.

The way to apply this model to sales is to practice one behavior in *every* sales call until the entire system is

95

automatically part of your selling behavior. This is where the daily behavior journal can be so valuable. Again, rather than practice one selling behavior in the first sales call, then a completely different sales behavior in the second call, and so on, instead we suggest that you pick one specific behavior and practice it in *every* sales call until you have mastered it. Chart your progress in your journal until you have consistently achieved the 7-10 range on that particular behavior. Then, and only then, begin to work on the next behavior, and continue this method until all of the desired changes have been made.

By using this approach, an interesting phenomenon occurs called "behavior clustering." What happens is that the behaviors begin to cluster together because they are all part of a "system." So even though you are concentrating on practicing one particular selling behavior at a time, other related behaviors unexpectedly "pop up" during the sales call, as if having appeared from thin air.

When such a revelation occurs, you may find yourself asking, "Where did that come from?" because in amazement you did something or said something that you hadn't expected, or planned. This is a definite indication that you are progressing in your learning curve, but don't let this occurrence derail your attempt to perfect the targeted behavior. Stay focused on practicing the selling behavior that you are charting in your journal. Over time this clustering effect forms the basis of the entire Leadership Selling system. Remember, you achieve mastery of that system by perfecting one skill at a time.

Step 5: Practice in Non-Selling Situations Also

Leadership Selling requires learning a method of communication that has broad applications. In addition to the fact that this system works well in a selling situation, you will find that the techniques and skills are highly efficient and tremendously effective communication tools to use in other situations, as well. As we said earlier, many people who adopt Leadership Selling report how much the skills they've learned have improved the quality of their lives outside of sales. This is because it tends to enhance their relationships with others in that it eliminates much of the confusion and misinterpretation that cause communication to break down.

The point is, the world can become your practice field once you are aware of the broad application of the techniques and skills inherent in the system. There is virtually no time when you are interacting with another human being that there isn't occasion to put one or more of the strategies to work. There is no excuse, then, for ever saying "I haven't had a chance to use it yet." The fact of the matter is that you rarely if ever have occasion *not* to use it.

Learning by Doing

It will help to implement your plan of action if you understand that there are natural, definable stages that everyone experiences when they work at changing their behavior, as shown in Figure 8.

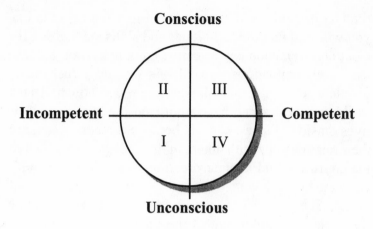

Figure 8

Quadrant I represents the stage at which we are **unconsciously incompetent,** meaning that we aren't good at doing something and we aren't aware that we aren't good at doing it. Once we learn the conceptual fundamentals of a desired behavior, we progress to quadrant II—**conscious incompetence**—where we aren't good at the new behavior and now we are aware of that fact. This can be an eye-opening and painful stage to go through because it isn't comfortable to admit when we are incompetent, even if it's temporary.

As we begin to practice the new behavior, we gradually improve until we move into quadrant III, or **conscious competence**. Here we are becoming proficient at the behavior, but only to the extent that we are consciously working at it. Eventually we repeat the new skill enough times that we reach quadrant IV—**unconscious competence**—where we master the behavior and no longer think about it in order to perform it well. Quadrant IV is the stage experienced drivers are in when they are driving. They see a stop light and stop without thinking; their behavior has become a reflex.

The Ultimate Goal

The ultimate goal with Leadership Selling is to achieve quadrant IV where you perform the techniques effortlessly. This is not to say that you should ever lose your ability to return to quadrant III periodically where the techniques are conscious, and therefore transferable. In fact, at times it is important to do so, such as when training a new member of the sales team. It is only to say that once in quadrant IV, you "own" the new behavior in that it has automatically become a part of you, which is the ideal. Again, this will take time to achieve because it involves changing behaviors, and this is why it is so important to develop a plan to ensure that the change actually occurs.

12

Having the Right Attitude

Now, more than ever before, salespeople must acquire a business owner's mentality if they hope to succeed. To one degree or another, salespeople have generally thought like owners in the sense that they have shared the mutual goal of generating a profit, just as they still do. But now that business is changing at warp speed, salespeople no longer have the luxury of receiving direction from management to the extent that they once did; managers simply don't have the time to do so. As a result, the sales profession is undergoing tumultuous change in that there is an epidemic need for all salespeople to manage their work-related activities from a business owner's perspective.

<u>*Areas That Must Be Managed*</u>

Just as owners carefully manage various categories of their fiscal affairs, so must salespeople manage various aspects of their job. Owners are responsible for overseeing four specific financial areas: cash flow, accounts receivable, inventory, and fixed assets. By comparison, salespeople must manage four similar areas that relate directly to their ability to generate profit: time, referrals, opportunities, and knowledge.

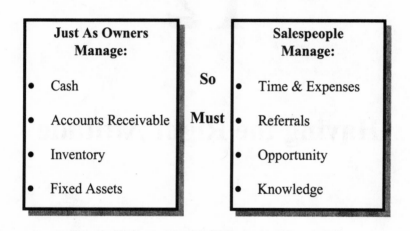

Just As Owners Manage:		**Salespeople Manage:**
• Cash	**So**	• Time & Expenses
• Accounts Receivable	**Must**	• Referrals
• Inventory		• Opportunity
• Fixed Assets		• Knowledge

<u>*The Similarities*</u>

<u>Cash = Time & Expenses</u>

The goal for a salesperson in regard to his time and expenses is identical to the goal of the business owner with his cash: *it should not be wasted!* In this sense, time is cash. Yet as previously discussed, customers waste untold hours of a salesperson's time when they are allowed to control the sales interaction with their own rules.

Again, this must stop, and adopting the attitude of a business owner helps toward this end.

Accounts Receivable = Referrals

Similarly with the salesperson's referrals and the business owner's accounts receivable, the goal is to keep them up to date. They are both money waiting to be collected—IOUs waiting to be cashed in. From this new point of view referrals, like accounts receivable, cannot be ignored or postponed. They are the pipeline of continuous profit.

Inventory = Opportunity

A salesperson's opportunity is akin to an owner's inventory in that the key is to turn them both over quickly. Inventory that isn't moved in a timely way is money poorly managed; a sales opportunity that isn't acted on immediately is money lost, because in sales elapsed time kills deals.

Fixed Assets = Knowledge

Knowledge and fixed assets must both be invested in wisely in order to maintain the period of time that they can be used effectively. In this sense it is important to be aware that Leadership Selling is not just another motivational fad or selling gimmick that is here today and gone tomorrow, like so many new ideas in sales tend to be. Rather, it is a fixed asset that pays dividends in the future.

Our honest prognosis is that those salespeople who act now to acquire the knowledge and implement the behaviors of Leadership Selling are sure to secure their future in sales, while those who don't will soon be left behind.

Salespeople who continue to use antiquated methods such as freely presenting features and benefits are likely to wake up one day realizing that their selling days are numbered unless they embark immediately on making the necessary behavioral change. The simple truth is that giving away free information depreciates its value and shortens its effective life span, two situations that would never be tolerated if viewed through a business owner's eyes.

Business Owners Act As Leaders

When a salesperson accepts the fact that he must approach selling with an owner's mentality, he is then officially in position to become a leader and execute Leadership Selling. With that in mind, let's look at the qualities that represent the true leader as summarized from our book, *Let's Get Results, Not Excuses!*

A (sales) leader must:

- **have vision.** He knows exactly where he wants to go and what he wants to accomplish. This means that he has clear sales goals and a clear plan of action to achieve them.

- **respect authority.** This relates to the accountability issue. By answering to an outside authority, a salesperson inherently respects the guidance of another person who can offer valuable feedback and share a fresh perspective on his sales efforts.

- **be self-confident.** Self-confidence is a direct outgrowth of self-esteem. If you don't believe that you are capable of success, you won't achieve it. And you must truly believe that you are capable of success if you plan to master Leadership Selling.

- **be enthusiastic.** Enthusiasm, self-confidence, high self-esteem, and optimism are all related concepts. Enthusiasm is infectious and attracts your customers to you. We caution you, however, that we do not mean enthusiasm in the traditional selling sense, namely getting all hyped-up about your product in the hope that your prospect will share your excitement. This kind of enthusiasm tends to frighten the buyer and cause him to question whether he can trust you. The type of enthusiasm that we intend is a quiet enthusiasm, one that conveys a sincere interest in helping the buyer to discover his problem and, with your help, solve it.

- **have a high energy level.** Energy is a direct descendent of the optimism of salespeople who are looking forward to, and who are focused on, the achievement of their goals. High energy, like enthusiasm, doesn't mean being excited and excitable with one's customers. It means rather that when a salesperson is in a difficult situation without much time to act, he can call on his energy, fire the afterburners, and go into hyperdrive speed to do whatever has to be done.

- **focus on the bigger picture.** Like the owner, salespeople must consider the entirety of their job and not let the small things distract them. For example, no salesperson likes to be rejected. Yet those individuals who stay focused on the bigger picture take isolated instances of rejection in stride, while those who don't stay focused on the bigger picture are more prone to get sidetracked in their feelings of dejection.

- **be proactive.** To "proact" is to have foresight rather than hindsight, and to do something purposeful that will yield a desired result. In sales, it is to lead the transaction rather than follow. "Proacting" is so important in Leadership Selling that Chapter 19 is given entirely to that subject.

- **expect success.** Good leaders create an expectation of success in whatever they undertake. Relative to sales, this means refusing to take "think it over's" or to "chase" customers precisely because both lead to eventual failure, which is not an option for a leader.

- **be self-disciplined.** No matter what the job, no matter what the task, there will always be elements that are distasteful. A sales leader does whatever it takes to get the job done, no matter how unpleasant the task may be at the time. The lack of self-discipline to undertake the undesirable aspects of one's job is one of the major common denominators of sales failure.

- **be willing to take risks.** Good leaders will take risks, and they will have the self-confidence to face the possibility of failure in order to reach their objectives. Risk-taking means being courageous—that is, being willing to engage in certain behaviors even though one may fear doing so. Whether it involves calling on the top person in an organization, confronting unacceptable situations with customers, or whatever one's fears happen to be, the courage to risk failure is one of the first attributes of a true sales leader.

- **be mentally tough and emotionally stable.** Leaders must keep going in the face of criticism and rejection; nothing deters them from the completion of their tasks.

Specifically in Leadership Selling, a salesperson must be mentally strong enough to ask the tough questions that customers would rather ignore, and be emotionally stable enough to work through the answers, whatever those answers happen to be.

- **recognize the need for additional knowledge.** While the majority of people resist change, a leader will keep abreast of innovative ideas. This relates back to the concept that knowledge is a fixed asset for salespeople who understand the importance of continuously acquiring it.

- **be a good listener.** The first sign of greatness in a leader is the ability to develop greatness in others. One cannot develop good leadership qualities in others unless he is able to listen to their ideas and opinions. Neither can one be a great salesperson until he is willing and able to listen to his customer's true problems, and subsequently help him solve them.

- **be "lucky."** Luck is defined as *when preparation meets with opportunity, and the opportunity is recognized and seized.* Sales leaders seize the moment when opportunity knocks, since again, time kills deals.

- **be introspective.** Leaders must continually look inward for areas of weakness that need to be improved. This is one reason that we emphasize how important the daily behavior journal can be for salespeople. It is a way to track their improvement on specific behaviors and leadership characteristics, ones about which they have introspected and subsequently targeted for change.

- **have integrity.** Sales leaders are honest, consistent, and trustworthy. Leadership Selling is impossible to execute without integrity, since customers do not trust salespeople who don't consistently demonstrate it.

- **have control.** There is nothing in all of sales more important than the ability to control the sales interaction, while at the same time allowing the buyer to believe that he is in control. Without establishing and maintaining control, it is impossible for a salesperson to lead a buyer in the sense that we mean "lead."

- **be decisive.** He who hesitates is lost, *especially* now that change occurs at warp speed. Leaders in the field of sales must not only be decisive themselves, they must also effectively communicate to their customers that decisiveness is expected of them, as well.

- **be a good communicator.** Traditionally, an effective communicator was one who was good at "telling," since to communicate meant to inform. Today, effective communication means *getting* information as much as giving it. Therefore, today's sales leaders must be more adept at asking than telling. Information is power; and a salesperson's ability to lead the customer in such a way as to gather necessary information makes him a good communicator, and, as a result, a top sales performer.

- **be sensitive.** Leaders understand the importance of keeping those whom they lead feeling OK. Since salespeople must lead the selling interaction, they must be sensitive to their customers' feelings and keep them feeling OK at all times—a subject we explore in detail in the following chapter.

Part IV

The Game Itself

THE GAME ITSELF is the heart and soul of Leadership Selling in that it unfolds the actual techniques that are essential to this revolutionary system. The eight parts of the Leadership Selling Compass correspond to the eight chapters in PART IV. The compass itself symbolizes two ideas. First, its circular shape represents the *integrity* and *universality* of Leadership Selling. Second, it serves as a reference point for a salesperson to determine where he is at any given moment in the sales process so that he can decide where next to lead the customer.

13

Keeping Your
Customer OK

A flurry of activity in recent years has been directed toward improving relationships with customers, especially as it concerns the process of bonding and establishing rapport. Many excellent books are available on these subjects, and we encourage you to stay familiar with such literature, including topics such as neurolinguistic programming, reading body language, understanding personality types, and so on. The truth is that professional salespeople can never know too much about human behavior and the psychology of the buyer.

That given, we will confine the discussion here to those aspects of relationship building that are especially germane to Leadership Selling. In particular, we will look at the importance of working on keeping your customer OK at all times.

Feeling OK Versus Feeling Not OK

If given the choice, normal people would naturally opt for the psychological state of feeling "OK" as opposed to feeling "not OK." OKness and not OKness are not absolute emotional states, of course, where a person feels totally one way or the other. Instead, one generally feels varying degrees of OKness or not OKness, depending on many internal and external factors.

Figure 9

Referring back to the self/behavior scale in Figure 5 (page 75), you can now see how self-esteem is actually measured in terms of how OK one feels about himself. That is, the more OK one feels about himself, the higher his self-esteem, and the less OK one feels about himself, the lower his self-esteem.

Trust and OKness

In general, people want to feel more OK about themselves than they actually feel most of the time. Feelings of OKness fluctuate constantly, and except in fleeting moments here and there, no one ever feels totally OK.

This concept can be used as a powerful selling tool. Since people in general want to feel more OK about themselves, they enjoy being in the presence of people who have the ability to help them achieve that psychological state. Feeling more OK is needed so much by most people, in fact, that customers are much more inclined to purchase from those salespeople who make them feel more OK than from those who do not. A good rule to follow is,

> *People bond with, and buy from, individuals whom they trust and like, and they trust and like salespeople who make them feel better, or more OK, about themselves.*

When a salesperson adopts this view, the challenge is to develop the necessary skills to keep his customers feeling OK as much of the time as possible. The more ability one develops in this department, the more customers he'll attract, and sell to. There may be no technique in all of sales that is more powerful than that of keeping buyers feeling OK about themselves. It is in essence the very nucleus of Leadership Selling, since people naturally follow those who make them feel more OK.

~

Before exploring the dos and don'ts of how to accomplish keeping your customer OK, let us be reminded that it is paramount for salespeople to work at maintaining their own high levels of self-esteem. It is difficult, if not impossible, to help other people feel OK if one doesn't feel OK about himself first. Otherwise, one is so busy struggling with his own self-esteem that keeping his customer OK may be the *last* thing on his mind. Moreover, since "one-upping" another person is one of the common ways that people with low self-esteem try to feel better about themselves, it is extremely counterproductive whenever a salesperson with low self-esteem tries to "one-up" his customer.

~

What follows, then, are four strategies for keeping your customer OK. Each by itself is highly effective; however, using all four in some combination is powerful!

Stamping

While it isn't popular to admit to the fact, if the truth be known every person's favorite subject is himself. People tend to like themselves more when they're talking than when they're listening. It is therefore important to get your customer talking as soon as possible in order to help him feel OK.

An amazingly easy way to achieve this is through the use of a process that we call "stamping." Essentially, stamping consists of three parts:

1. Find something in your customer that you share an interest in, be it a person, place, or thing.

2. Acknowledge the fact that you share that interest in common with him, which in effect gives him your stamp of approval.

3. Ask your customer to tell you about *his* interest or experience as opposed to you telling him about your own.

The reason why stamping works so well as a selling tool is that it is exactly the opposite of what usually happens in social discourse. Let's say that you're at a social gathering and you bring up a recent car accident that you had. Before you know it, the other person proceeds to elaborate about the last time that he wrecked his car. How did that make you feel? How do you think it makes a customer feel when it happens to him? We've all been there, and we all know what a turn-off it can be. It's the old "You think your operation was bad, wait until you hear what happened to me" syndrome.

The above scenario shows how *not* to stamp. To the contrary, when someone says something that you can relate to—say golfing, for example—you now would practice stamping by saying, "I like to golf, too. *Tell* me about *your* golf game."

An Example

Jack was the owner of a small consulting business and had an appointment with Tom in a city about a one-hour drive away. As he was driving to his meeting, he suddenly experienced excrutiating lower back pain. Not knowing what else to do, Jack decided to exceed the speed limit in hopes of attracting the attention of a police officer, who could assist by transporting Jack to the nearest emergency room. That didn't happen, however, and the pain intensified as it spread to his lower abdomen. The pain was so unbearable that, in hindsight, it was a sheer miracle that Jack didn't pass out while intentionally speeding.

Fortunately, he was able to reach his original destination, where Tom noticed from his office window that Jack was doubled over with pain and was ashen colored as he stumbled slowly out of his car. Tom went immediately to help; and when he realized how much Jack was suffering, he helped him into the car and speeded to the emergency room of the nearest hospital.

Four hours later, Jack painfully passed a kidney stone. He was subsequently released from the hospital, totally spent from the trauma and the pain of the whole ordeal. He returned to his office, still wearing his hospital admittance bracelet.

As he unlocked his office door, a copy machine salesman whom Jack had never seen before unexpectedly approached him. Jack was in no mood to talk copiers; but after a brief hello, the salesman inquired as to why he was wearing the hospital ID tag. Jack started to explain that earlier in the day he had passed a kidney stone, but the salesman soon interrupted: "I know exactly what that's like—I had a kidney stone ten years ago myself! Let me tell you about it. I was driving in the car, and the pain was so bad that I had to recline the seat as far as it would go in order to straighten my back. I could barely see over the dashboard, I had never felt so much pain, I thought my life was over, and blah, blah, blah."

Jack was appalled. The last thing in the world that he wanted to hear about was the salesman's kidney stone ordeal from ten years ago. Jack was not OK *before* the salesman walked in; he was even less OK afterward.

What the salesman in the story did was the exact opposite of "stamping." Jack needed the salesman to say something like, "Oh no, I'm so sorry to hear that! I had a kidney stone once, and I know you've just been through a lot of pain. Please tell me what happened."

Had the salesman done this, he would have been using the bonding technique we refer to as stamping. He would have acknowledged that they shared a similar experience, and then he would have listened to Jack and let him talk about the pain that he had just gone through.

Incidentally, Jack was in the market for a new copier, but he certainly didn't buy from the salesman who talked about his own kidney stone ordeal. Had the salesman known how to stamp properly, he might well have made a sale that day, or soon thereafter.

When to Stamp, and on Which Subjects

As for what subjects one can use to stamp, use good judgment, of course. It may be a family picture in the prospect's office, or an award or plaque on his wall. It may be a topic that comes up in the conversation—especially as an ice-breaker early on, which is the best time to stamp—about kids, or fishing, or a favorite athletic team. By and large, the closer the subject is to the buyer's heart, the more you are building his "OKness," which is your ultimate goal.

Stroking

Psychologically speaking, a "stroke" is an affirmation, such as a compliment or a statement of praise. Stroking is an excellent way to keep your customer OK. It helps him see himself through the positive lens of your comment rather than through the often-negative tone that he hears either from others, or from his own self-talk. Remember, the customer who feels OK about himself as a result of being with you is far more likely to buy from you than from another salesperson who doesn't know how to help him feel this way.

There are two categories of stroking: obvious or overt stroking, and subtle or covert stroking. Of the two, the latter is much more powerful because it is less obvious to the customer, and is therefore much more difficult for him to detect. Both, however, are important and should be equally mastered.

Obvious or Overt Stroking

Everyone appreciates a sincere compliment from another human being, even if it appears that they are uncomfortable receiving it at the time. "You look nice today," or "You did a terrific job on that project," or "I enjoy doing business with you" are excellent examples of comments that keep people feeling OK. We tend to forget in the workaday and often negative world exactly how frequently people need positive strokes on an ongoing basis.

Unfortunately, some fast-talking salespeople have tried to use this principle to their advantage by stroking customers even if the compliment is insincere. Such individuals seem to approach human relations with a "flattery will get me everywhere" attitude. The problem is that customers tend to be wary of salespeople who over-compliment them, so much so, in fact, that it usually back-fires in the salesperson's face.

So long as your strokes are meaningful, appropriate, and sincere, they go a long way toward keeping your customer feeling OK. Otherwise, he will smell your insincerity from the proverbial "mile away," and he will dismiss you accordingly. To play it safe, it's a good idea to use overt strokes sparingly, and only when your compliment is sincere.

Subtle or Covert Stroking

Again, the less obvious to the customer that your efforts are at stroking, the more powerful it is in terms of keeping them feeling OK. The goal with covert stroking is to deliver the compliment in such a way that customers don't recognize that you are, in fact, stroking them.

To accomplish subtle stroking, it helps to understand the whole matter of human intentionality. With rare exceptions, *most people have good intentions most of the time.* That is, most people intend well regardless of the outcome of their actions.

Knowing this, an entire communication pattern for responding to customers' dialogue is possible that has the cumulative effect of making them feel more OK. The difference between obvious stroking and subtle stroking is that in the second case, you are purposely complimenting a person's intentions as opposed to their actions. Examples include, but are certainly not limited to, such brief expressions as:

- "That's a great suggestion!"

- "Thank you for bringing that up."

- "I'm glad you asked."

119

- "Good idea!"

- "Precisely!"

- "Exactly!"

- "I couldn't have said that better myself."

- "That's an excellent question."

- "What a valuable idea!"

- "I agree."

The power of these statements is, of course, in what they imply about the worth of the customer. If the customer asks, "What about such-and-such?" and the next words out of your mouth are, "That's an excellent question," you have sent him a subtle message that he is an excellent person for having asked this question. Similarly, if your customer raises a concern and you respond with "I'm glad you brought that up," you have in effect said to him that he has a question or a thought that is worth a lot, and that therefore, so is he.

Subtle Stroking Is Invisible

There is no end to the possibilities for using these kinds of subtle affirmations with customers. Since they are brief, used often, and feel so good to the customer that he doesn't pause to figure out *why* he feels good, they go mostly unnoticed by him. Consequently, subtle strokes are excellent statements for you to use to keep your customers feeling OK during *all* buyer/seller interactions.

Two other thoughts on the subject of covert stroking. First, people want to be treated as unique and special—one of a kind—when they do or say something positive, and every comment on the preceding list does precisely that. It's helpful to know, however, that when people hurt in some way—that is, when they are experiencing something negative in their lives—they want to feel that they're not alone with their problem. Therefore, if a customer said to you, "Things are pretty rough right now," it would be inappropriate to respond with "I'm glad you brought that up" or "Good job!" To keep this customer feeling OK, you must let him know that he is part of a larger group with a comment like "You're not the first person who said that to me today," or "I've been hearing that a lot lately," or something to that effect. This satisfies his need to not feel alone in his discomfort.

Second, one of the quickest ways to help your customer feel OK, especially if you're sensing that he's not, is to ask him the question directly, "Are you OK?" If he's not, he'll probably tell you so, thereby giving you the opportunity to correct whatever is making him feel not OK; if he is, it registers in his unconscious that you are *concerned* about his OKness, which by itself helps keep him feeling more OK. Caution should be exercised, of course, to not overuse the question because overuse can become irritating and might imply that you didn't believe the customer's response the first time.

Struggling

One of the foremost ways that people use to measure their OKness is to compare themselves with others. The less OK those around us seem to feel, the more OK it seems like we are in comparison.

As an example, parents are often upset about the friends that their teenage children associate with for precisely this reason. Adolescence is an age of much floundering and searching for one's identity, and "hanging out" with friends who feel less OK assures a teen that he himself is OK, because so often he feels that he is not.

Salespeople have long been taught to put their best foot forward, to display confidence, to act as if all were well and nothing ever bothered them—in short, to "act sharp, feel sharp, and be sharp." The problem is that this air of confidence in the salesperson can be easily perceived as arrogance by the customer who, as we said, is likely feeling less-than-totally-OK himself. The net effect is that the customer tends to feel inferior in his presence and may even shun this type of salesperson because he doesn't want to relate with people who make him feel not OK. The result: no sale.

By contrast, if the salesperson acts less OK than the customer (and we emphasize *acts* less OK rather than *feels* less OK, since salespeople must maintain a high level of self-esteem), the customer *in relation to the salesperson* feels more OK, which, again, is the goal.

A Role Model for Acting Not OK

An excellent way to understand the power of struggling is to observe the popular television detective "Columbo" as played by Peter Falk. While it is not necessary that salespeople dress in a frumpy raincoat, drive a beat-up old car, own a sad and pitiful-looking dog, act clumsy, and smoke cigars, it is *absolutely* necessary that they use much of his vocabulary. Those who are familiar with the program will know that Columbo always gets his man, although he often acts like a bumbling idiot while in pursuit of his suspect. Actually, he's dumb like a fox. The reason he's so effective is that he always keeps his suspects feeling very OK, hence they let down their guard at some point, and invariably he catches them in a lie.

Let's take a closer look at some of Columbo's common phrases to better understand examples of struggling:

- "I'm sorry, sir."

- "Do you mind if I ask you another question?"

- "Could you please repeat that, ma'am?"

- "Help me understand that better if you would."

- "I'm sure any misunderstanding was my fault."

- "I'm very confused, sir; help me if you will."

- "Oh, well that explains it, sir; thank you very much."

- "Excuse me, please; I didn't mean to interrupt."

- "Forgive me for intruding, if you will."

- "I'm sure you're right about that, sir."

Notice that every one of these remarks automatically, but not in any way that is obvious, places Columbo in the *inferior* position, while clearly placing his suspect in the *superior* position. That is, each comment makes it seem as if Columbo is less OK, thus positioning his suspect to feel more OK *than he*. In turn, the suspect is not threatened, and therefore opens up and tells all.

This is exactly the goal in Leadership Selling. The object is to get the customer to open up and reveal his true buying motive—that is, his problem or his pain that he is otherwise by nature reluctant to share. Once he opens up, you have a much better chance to sell him your product or service as the solution to his problem, assuming of course that what you sell does provide an answer.

Examples of Struggling

One of the greatest techniques available to accomplish this is to master the art of struggling. When your customer says something that is contradictory, don't say, "It seems to me that you just contradicted yourself." This is the way to make him feel not OK very quickly! Instead, say, "I'm a little confused by such-and-such. Could you help me understand that better?" By going not OK on him, your customer will attempt to rescue you, and thereby clear up his own contradiction. People almost always try to rescue someone who goes suddenly not OK on them; and part of their rescue effort is to give you what you need, even if it's valuable information that they wouldn't otherwise offer.

Another example is, if something goes wrong and it is obviously the customer's mistake, you take the blame for it rather than allow him to feel not OK. Even if it's clearly his error, you apologize, just as Columbo would. For example, if your customer forgets an appointment, don't say, "You forgot our appointment." Instead, say, "I was there for our appointment, but when you didn't show up, I figured that I'd made a mistake." This will keep him OK and he will continue to work with you. In fact, he may even feel indebted to you and end up buying for that reason alone.

None of this is to say that you should allow yourself to be treated like a doormat by your customers. Quite the opposite is true. But it is to say that by changing your phraseology to "I'm not OK" terms, you will make the customer feel more OK. And because that psychological state is so important to everyone, he will unknowingly cooperate with you in ways that he himself would never have dreamed possible.

KISS

We've all heard that it's important in life to Keep It Simple, Stupid. Our version of this acronym is Keep It Simple, Salesperson, which is the fourth technique for keeping your customer OK.

One of the ways that salespeople often make their customers feel not OK is by using the jargon that is basic to their industry—the "buzzwords" of the trade, if you will. This can be extemely dangerous in terms of making people feel not OK, since buzzwords are not easily or readily understood by customers. It's not unlike how one feels when people speak a different language in front of him—naive and somewhat stupid.

John F. Kennedy was one of the most popular presidents in the history of the United States. One of the standards that he demanded from all of his speechwriters was that they use terms that the average sixth-grader could understand. He did this to make his audience feel OK.

This is an appropriate rule for salespeople to follow, as well. MODs, PPQs, RVTs, OEMs, PIVs, Fannie Mays, APRs—nothing makes a person feel more uncomfortable than a buzzword thrown at them that they don't understand. Rather than respond by saying, "I don't know what that means," many people feel embarrassed that they don't know, and subsequently, they feel very not OK. Once this occurs, the chances are high that the prospective customer will try to avoid the salesperson in one way or another. In this sense, the use of industry jargon can defeat the entire purpose of the sales interaction.

Salespeople are notorious for committing this error, partly out of habit since they hear the words so often themselves, and partly out of their own attempts to feel OK (the old I-know-more-than-you-on-this-subject syndrome). For whatever reason this has occurred, in order to do Leadership Selling, all such behavior must be monitored very closely.

When to Use Buzzwords

A handy principle to adopt in this regard is to only use buzzwords under two conditions: either when your customer uses them first, which means that he understands the terms; or when you pause after you use a buzzword and explain its meaning. "The ANR—annual net return—with this company has become quite predictable," and so on. Even then, the only real reason to do the latter is to educate the buyer without making him feel not OK if in your judgment it's important for him to learn that particular term. Otherwise it is best to speak to customers just as JFK spoke to his audiences. That way you intentionally keep them OK with the terminology that you use.

Some salespeople at this point have wondered if these four techniques—stamping, stroking, struggling, and KISS—aren't manipulative, thereby suggesting that they might be unethical strategies to use with customers. The answer lies in your intentions; remember, you aren't employing these skills for purely selfish reasons. You are getting the customer to open up to you about matters that he instinctively wants to keep hidden. The reason you want to do this is so that you can determine if you can help him with his problem or not. It would be unethical to sell him something that he doesn't really need just so you can make a profit.

Acquiring the ability to do this represents the very pinnacle of professionalism in sales. The methods that you use to attain such professionalism are the tools of your trade, and they are not to be viewed as unethical any more than a doctor's scalpel by itself is unethical. It's how one uses his professional tools that counts. When a doctor uses his scalpel to perform unnecessary operations to reap unwarranted profits, that's being manipulative. However, when he uses it to carefully and skillfully remove a malignant tumor, that's quite another issue, even though it also generates a respectable profit.

So it is with strategies designed to keep your customer OK. They are tools that you can use in order to best perform your professional service. It is up to you to make sure that you use them ethically.

Keeping your customer OK is the very first step on your new selling journey. It is important to understand, however, that this is not something that you do one time with your customers and then consider it finished.

The challenge of making sure that your customer is OK is a never-ending job. You should start the process from the moment you first meet a prospective customer, and you should never stop as long as your business relationship continues to exist.

The bottom line is that keeping your customer OK is an essential ingredient for skillfully performing every step that follows in the Leadership Selling system. The sooner you master how to do it, the better you will be at executing the system.

14

Setting the New Rules

You will recall from Part II that buyers and sellers each have a system; that the buyer's system is *vastly* more powerful than the traditional seller's system; and that salespeople must learn how to play a new game by a whole new set of rules. That is, they must drastically change the way they approach the entire selling process if they hope to thrive in the warp-speed economy in which we live.

Most sales interactions begin without a conscious effort by either party to establish the rules for how to proceed, which means that the buyer's rules (feign interest, steal information, stall for time while promising to get back, and then ignore the salesperson) are automatically in effect *by default*. This is because the rules of the more powerful buyer's system dominate the entire interaction unless specific measures are implemented by the seller to reverse the process and take the lead position.

The Seller Must Take Charge Immediately

Selling is like an athletic event in that it is important to begin with a discussion about the rules by which the contest will proceed. The next time you attend a sporting event, pay special attention to the meeting that occurs immediately before the beginning of the game. Baseball games are preceded by a meeting at home plate between the umpires and the managers; football games by a meeting at midfield between the referees and the captains; boxing matches by a meeting at center ring between the fighters and the referee. In each situation, the purpose of the meeting is to establish the rules by which the game is to be played.

Similarly, the rules must be established up front between a seller and a buyer before heading into the selling interaction. We call this "establishing an upfront contract." In essence, an upfront contract, or agreement, helps answer the questions "Why are we here?" and "What are we trying to accomplish?" so that all parties involved are operating with a common purpose in mind.

But there is a clear difference between selling events and athletic events. Since there is no referee involved, *you must act as the referee* by taking the initiative to discuss the rules at the very outset of the interaction. Again, if you don't discuss the rules, neither will the buyer; yet his rules will automatically prevail. This is because he *expects* you to follow his rules, since that precedent has been clearly established and rarely challenged over time.

Remember, since customers buy to solve a problem, you are about to lead the buyer into emotionally uncomfortable territory. He is going to resist your attempts to do this unless you have some clear agreements with him about how you both should proceed. His first act of resistance will be to superimpose his set of rules onto the transaction without actually stating or verbalizing his intentions. In fact, since the buyer's process is automatic and unconscious, he doesn't even know that he's trying to take immediate control of the situation; it is something he does instantaneously, and without forethought. His attitude, remember, is "You need me more than I need you," so he naturally assumes that he gets to "call the shots."

Establishing the Rules Is a Three-Step Process

Step One

Your ability to perform the techniques in Leadership Selling will depend primarily on asking your customer many important and penetrating questions. Customers are the ones who expect to ask questions and to manipulate the salesperson into giving away free information. They will therefore experience it as an abrupt change for you to turn this around by 180° when you begin to ask the questions and they have to surrender the information.

The way to accomplish this with the least resistance possible is to request your customer's permission to ask him questions. This helps him to maintain his feeling of control, which is very important. Again, the buyer's system exists to help him feel in control of the interaction and to avoid being taken advantage of by the seller. In order for you to effectively take control and lead the conversation, it is important that you do this in a way that allows the customer to *feel* that he is in control, even though you are actually the one who is controlling the sales call from beginning to end.

There can be some flexibility in the way that you carry out Step One, depending on your personality, speech patterns, and individual communication style. At the center of your message, however, must be these words, or their equivalent: "I will need to ask you several questions; will that be okay?" People invariably answer "yes" to this question. On those extremely rare occasions when they say "no," it's usually because they're in a hurry and don't have the time, in which case you simply ask them, "When would be a better time?" and then set up an appointment to meet at a later date.

Step Two

Naturally, customers will have questions to ask of you. They must be reassured that it is certainly appropriate for them to ask questions, too. Even though this could easily be assumed, giving the buyer permission to ask whatever is on his mind reduces his fears and lets him feel that he has control of the interaction.

The words needed to convey this point are pretty straightforward. You simply say something to the effect of "I expect that you will have some questions, as well, and I want you to feel free to ask me anything that you would like to know."

Step Three

The purpose of stating that you are going to ask the customer some questions, and then to give him permission to ask you questions, is to determine (1) whether or not the two of you have anything further to talk about, and (2) whether it makes the most sense to "stop" or "move forward" in your interaction together.

Accordingly, that's exactly what you say to the customer. Let him feel comfortable that you're not asking him to make a decision as to whether he's going to buy before you've answered each other's questions. You are simply wanting to know if, *after you have talked*, he will be able to tell you whether or not it makes sense to continue.

The reason this step is so important is that it supplants stages three and four of the buyer's system. It is in those stages, you will recall, that buyers tend to trap the seller into the gray area of "maybe," "I want to think it over," "I need to talk to my boss," or any of several other common stalls that people use to get rid of salespeople.

Buyers have long been able to get away with this strategy because salespeople have allowed them to get away with it. Traditionally, it seems that the best answer a salesperson can hear from a customer is "yes," the second best answer is some form of "let me think it over," and the most dreaded answer is "no." Because salespeople have been afraid to hear a customer say "no," they have been willing to accept "think-it-overs" (hereafter referred to as "TIOs").

The problem with this, as we said previously, is that the vast majority of TIOs really mean no; yet since salespeople don't want to hear no, they'd rather accept a TIO. This sets the seller up for step four of the traditional selling system—namely, to chase the customer who said he'd get back, but does not. As a result, salespeople waste tremendous amounts of time chasing suspects rather than working with prospects—time that they can no longer afford to waste!

In summary, then, the three steps for establishing

an upfront contract include:

> 1. **Get permission from the buyer to ask him questions.**
>
> 2. **Give the buyer permission to ask you questions.**
>
> 3. **Gently inform the customer that you expect him to make a decision at the end as to whether he wants to stop or continue.**

Acceptable Responses from the Customer in Leadership Selling

The new priority, therefore, in terms of answers that salespeople can accept from customers, is as follows:

- the best answer a salesperson can hear from a customer is, of course, "yes"

- the second best answer is "no"

- the worst possible answer is some form of "TIO"

The truth is that TIOs must not be tolerated any longer! *No more "Think It Overs," period!* They must be eliminated and replaced with either "yes's" (that is, "yes we will move forward"), or "no's" (that is, "no, it's over"). This way, the suspects get sorted out from the prospects, and selling efficiency improves tremendously, as well as the results.

The best way to prevent TIOs is by using Step Three of the upfront contract. That is, ask the customer at the beginning of the sales interview, rather than at the end, if he'll know *and be willing to tell you* if he can make a decision today—either way—as to whether it's over or whether he wants to go further in the interaction.

As for the actual words, you say something on the order of, "When we finish talking, will you know at that point whether or not you will want to move forward or stop?" If a customer answers "yes" to this question, you have a clear upfront contract with him—which means that you have clearly established the rules, and you are well on your way to controlling the sales call.

If on the other hand he says "no" or "I'm not sure," then you'd want to ask him what would be required in order for him to know. In essence, he is indicating that he has an objection to continuing, and it is much better to find this out early on than after your presentation. Whatever he answers indicates some problem, and therefore must become the next topic of discussion until the rules for proceding are clear. *Never proceed in a sales interview until the rules for that interaction are clear and agreed upon.*

An Example

Usually when you ask a customer if he will be able to tell you at the conclusion whether he wants to move forward or stop, he will readily answer "yes." If on the other hand he responds that he doesn't know yet, he may be feeling pressured that he has to decide to buy before you even begin your discussion. In this case, struggle a little by apologizing for not having been clear in what you intended to say, then restate that you're not asking him to decide to purchase *before* the discussion, but rather that he will be willing to tell you *at the end* of the discussion if he has enough information to be able to make a decision.

A helpful tip to relax the buyer at this point is to inform him that "It is okay to say no." You would certainly appreciate that if you were in the buyer's position, would you not? So tell him. This also gives him the feeling that he is in control, which, again, is extremely important to do in Leadership Selling.

The problem arises in the salesperson's attitude toward telling a customer that it's okay to say no. "No" is the *last* thing he wants to hear, so he avoids like the plague telling the customer that "no" is okay. In fact, many salespeople have been taught by their managers *never* to accept a "no," so this concept may appear almost radical on the surface. But remember, in Leadership Selling a "no" is *much* better than getting a TIO. It takes inner strength, and you must discipline yourself in the beginning to give customers permission to say it in order to preclude their use of TIOs.

Interestingly enough, giving customers permission to say no becomes relatively easy to do in a short period of time. First, when you tell someone that it's okay to say no and then he actually says it, his "no" doesn't hurt nearly so much as it might otherwise; in fact, the whole exchange becomes a matter of mutual respect.

Second, and paradoxically:

> **The more you give customers permission to tell you "no," the less likely they are to actually say it.**

Just the fact that you care enough about them to bring the subject up allows them to relax and get involved in the interview in a more honest way. Since they have permission to tell you no, they don't have to spend so much of their time trying to figure out how to get rid of you, and they can actually communicate in a much more relaxed and honest manner. The result is often a sale where a sale might not have otherwise occurred.

Upfront Contracts Reviewed

If the whole idea of establishing the rules of the game up front seems tedious, it is only because it takes more time to explain each step than it takes to actually perform it. In practice, it takes only a few seconds, and is as simple and brief as saying:

> *"If it's all right with you, I'd like to ask you some questions—would that be okay?"* (Step One)

> *"And I'm sure you have some questions that you'd like to ask me, which I want you to feel free to do."* (Step Two)

> *"I'm wondering also if, after we've answered each other's questions, you'll feel comfortable at that point telling me one of two things—either that you have no interest in my product—which is perfectly acceptable—or that you'd like to look further into it together."* (Step Three)

Establishing the rules by setting an upfront contract is as simple as that! Yet it's as important as it is simple because it is a distinct and calculated move on your part to make the switch from following the buyer's powerful rules to leading with your own rules. By doing so, the entire sales interaction can proceed down a new pathway—*your* pathway—that gives you the decided advantage to close more deals and earn more money.

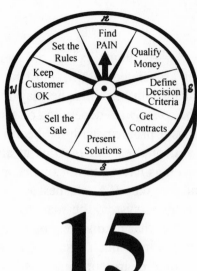

15

Discovering the Buyer's PAIN

You will recall from Chapter 1 that the only reason people buy anything is to solve some problem that they have. It is time now to understand more thoroughly the selling power that results from knowing how to uncover the buyer's problems, and the skills required to do so.

The Concept of PAIN

Whenever a person has a problem of any kind,

there is always—without exception—an underlying painful emotion associated with it. For example, if a parent has a problem with his child, he may feel *frustrated*, *angry*, or maybe *concerned*, depending on the situation. If an individual has a problem with his health, he may feel *worried, anxious,* or even *exasperated* at any related inconvenience, such as having to miss work, not being able to exercise, and the like. If a salesperson needs help with developing a referral system, he may feel *stressed* over having to do a task that he dislikes, or he may even feel *afraid* of losing his job. Each instance, as with all problems, involves some degree of inner discomfort or emotional stress.

All such emotional discomfort, distress, even "hurt," if you will, will hereafter be referred to as "PAIN"—an acronym for:

Problems

Anxieties

Irritations

Negative Feelings

All living creatures, and especially human beings, attempt to seek pleasure and avoid PAIN. Of the two, eliminating or preventing PAIN is by far the more powerful motivator. It could be argued, in fact, that since pleasure is a momentary PAINless state, even the pursuit of pleasure is the attempt to escape PAIN.

To suggest, then, that people buy to solve a specific problem is to say that people purchase solutions to get rid of, or to prevent, feeling PAIN. The goal for all salespeople in Leadership Selling, therefore, is to proactively seek out their prospective customer's PAIN; and, once revealed, to sell him a solution, and thereby generate a profit.

Buyers Tend to Disguise Their PAIN

The trouble is, getting people to expose their PAIN is not that simple to do. It is basic human nature to hide inner PAIN, first from oneself, and therefore necessarily from others. This is the function of denial, avoidance, and suppression—namely, to keep PAIN from entering into human consciousness so that one can escape actually feeling it.

As this principle relates to selling, buyers don't walk around broadcasting their PAIN freely. To the contrary, they do everything in their power to keep it hidden from the salesperson.

The way buyers do this is by wrapping their PAIN in layers of intellectual insulation:

Intellectual Layers of Defense

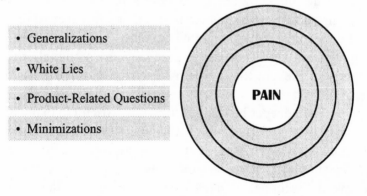

- Generalizations

- White Lies

- Product-Related Questions

- Minimizations

Figure 10

These layers may consist of **generalizations** like "I might be interested," **white lies** like "I'm just looking," **product-related questions** like "What's the life expectancy of your product?" and **minimizations** like "It's no big deal—I can live with it or without it."

Buyers use these intellectual defenses—one or in combination—to block salespeople from discovering their PAIN, that is, their true buying motives. Leadership Selling can be described as a process for leading buyers to systematically lower these natural defenses, and thereby become less resistant.

Examples of How Buyers Defend Themselves Against Feeling PAIN

Buyers are so well protected against feeling PAIN that even the ways in which they describe their own PAIN are designed to numb it. Ask someone who has stopped at a service station to buy gasoline *why* he did so, and you will likely hear him answer something like, "I was running low on gas," or "The gas gauge was registering near empty," or "I needed gas." All of these statements are no doubt true, but they represent only a *portion* of what is true. In each case, the answer is strictly an intellectual one that is devoid of any emotional content. Yet the *real* reason for stopping to buy gas is precisely an emotional one, namely to prevent the problems that would develop were he to run out.

Such deeper buying motives are difficult to express because they are usually hidden deep within, often even from his own awareness. Yet if he were able to verbalize his *true* buying motive, he would say, "I put gas in the tank to avoid the consequences of running out on the way home—arriving home late for dinner, walking miles to the nearest phone, being stranded in sub-zero weather," and so on. Granted, people are not socialized to talk this way; nevertheless, the point is that he stopped for gas to *prevent* PAIN. Again, this is one of the two reasons why anyone ultimately buys anything: to prevent PAIN or relieve PAIN.

Larry has just been abandoned by his wife and two children. She took most of their material possessions with her, including their only vehicle. Distraught, he boards a bus to the nearest car dealership to buy a car. The salesperson greets him and asks how he's doing, to which he politely responds "Fine" (which is a white lie). Then the seller inquires as to how he can help him, and Larry routinely replies, "I'm just looking," which is a generalization of his true situation.

It is certainly true that he is in fact looking, but not *just* looking, as if he were only remotely "interested." The truth is that he has a great deal of PAIN, but he isn't about to admit that to the salesman. He doesn't want to appear vulnerable for fear of being taken advantage of, so he acts strong and hides his PAIN.

Karen stopped by a real estate office to inquire about the price of a particular house that she liked. The realtor gave her the price, and then inquired if she were thinking about buying a home. "Perhaps," Karen replied guardedly. "I'm thinking about listing my own house and looking for another place to live."

The truth is that Karen has a growing family and is terribly cramped in her current home. There are too few bedrooms, not enough closet space, inadequate bathroom facilities, and a dining room that is too small to accommodate the entire family. Karen is in PAIN, yet to the realtor she only reveals that she is *thinking about* looking for another place. Again, this is because it is natural and normal for Karen to minimize her problems both to herself and to others.

The Salesperson's Challenge

Given that people tend to hide their true PAIN from the very people who can help them relieve it, the salesperson's job in Leadership Selling is much like the psychiatrist's job during therapy. Both must learn to carefully and expertly penetrate the layers of defense—the generalizations, the white lies, and so on—to get to the real source of their "client's" PAIN. And both must rely on their professional skills for keeping the person OK while still drawing out his PAIN.

To some readers the concept of keeping the customer OK while drawing out his PAIN may sound contradictory. How does one help a customer find his PAIN, which is obviously uncomfortable for him, yet still keep him feeling OK?

This is a very technical point. The key is to understand that PAIN and low self-esteem are not equivalent. A person can have high or low self-esteem and yet be in or out of PAIN. Knowing this, the idea is to treat your customer with respect and dignity, acknowledging at all times his OKness, even though you are at the same time trying to help him uncover his PAIN.

The Salesperson's Tools

As mentioned, buyers instinctively disguise their PAIN by withholding potentially "incriminating" information. The salesperson must develop the necessary skills to gain access to that information if he hopes to solve the problem by selling a solution to the prospective buyer. The way that he's going to penetrate the layers that protect the PAIN is by asking the right questions, which is the equivalent of a surgeon using a scalpel to get to the source of his patient's problem.

We are well aware, of course, that to ask probing questions of the customer is not a new concept in sales. It is our belief, however, that other selling systems have not placed *nearly* enough emphasis on the reality that (1) customers withhold information initially, and (2) in order to discover the customers' true buying motives, the salesperson must skillfully lead them through their own intellectual layers of defense in order to find their real PAIN.

To assist you in this regard, we will introduce twenty-two PAIN-finding rules. There will be instances where the rules overlap one another slightly, but don't let this confuse you. It is our intention that you look at PAIN from many different perspectives, and it is to be expected that there will be similarities between certain rules.

Rules for Finding the Customer's PAIN

PAIN Rule #1

Keep your customer talking.

The most effective way to get someone to talk is by asking him questions. In traditional selling, the philosophy has always been that "sellin' is tellin'." It is not uncommon when using this "show and tell" approach for salespeople to talk as much as 75 percent of the time, or even more.

In Leadership Selling, it is the direct opposite. The salesperson's goal is to *get* information much more than he *gives* it, hence he must be listening to the customer 75 percent of the time and talking the remaining 25 percent. Some individuals may worry that this doesn't give them enough time in a sales call to cover the required material. Yet 25 percent of an hour is still 15 minutes, and one can say a lot in 15 minutes!

PAIN Rule #2

Keep the focus on the customer's problem.

The customer will use different tactics to try to divert you away from his PAIN. He might:

- talk about unrelated topics

- change the focus onto price

- lead you down blind alleys

- skirt the real issue

- sidetrack you with tangents

You must be vigilant to ensure that this doesn't

happen if you expect to keep control of the sales call. Within reason, of course, continue to maintain control by using the appropriate questions to keep the conversation moving in the direction of his PAIN.

PAIN Rule #3

Answer the customer's questions sparingly.

A customer's inquiries accomplish two important objectives for him. First, and as mentioned, they are an effective way to intellectualize and therefore guard against his PAIN. Second, his questions manipulate the salesperson into the position of responding with valuable information that the customer can steal.

The truth is that whenever a customer asks a question, at some deeper level he is raising a red flag that says "There is PAIN beneath this question." It is your job to determine what is prompting his specific inquiry.

Let's suppose, for example, that you sell corporate health insurance benefits. Your prospect may ask, "How soon could the new policy take effect?" What he is actually doing is collecting information in the hope of solving a problem that he'd rather not reveal. Perhaps the situation is that his benefits are inadequate or have expired, either of which would give the impression that he was irresponsible. Rather than openly admit this, however, he protects himself and hides his PAIN by asking a product-related question.

The worst thing that you could do at this juncture would be to answer his question directly. Suppose you immediately responded by saying, "The policy would take effect one month from the date that you enroll." By doing this, the prospect has acquired valuable information from you, yet you missed a perfect opportunity to find out *why* he was asking the question. You have no idea whether he wants the policy to take effect sooner than one month, or later. Therefore, by answering his question too early, you may have, in effect, shot yourself in the foot in that he can now use that information as a reason not to buy from you.

PAIN Rule #4

Reverse your customer's questions.

To reverse anything is to turn it in the opposite direction. To reverse your customer's question specifically is to turn it in the opposite direction by *asking* a question of him rather than *answering* his question directly.

Remember, product-related questions from your customer are protective devices that he uses to insulate himself against revealing his real PAIN to you. Assuming that he has a specific PAIN, the customer believes that he has found a viable solution, so he asks product-related questions of you looking for confirmation. Once having received your free information and expert advice, he is then able to shop around and compare prices. Instead of acting like an unpaid consultant by giving away information, your job is to probe deeper into the "whys" of his questions to determine the source of his PAIN. The way to do this is to answer his questions with other questions. For example:

Customer: "What do you have?"

SP: "I'd be happy to show you, but I have so much information, what would you like to see?"

or

Customer: "How much RAM does your computer have?"

SP: "How much do you need?"

or

Customer: "How long will this particular product design be available on the market?"

SP: "May I ask your reason for wondering about that?"

PAIN Rule #5

Soften before you reverse.

Answering a question with a question can sometimes appear harsh to the customer. To prevent this from happening and to make sure that your customer stays OK, it is essential that you precede your next question with a psychological stroke which acts as a buffer. In each of the following cases, for example, the softening statement is *italicized* and precedes the reverse:

• *"Thank you for asking.* Is there a particular reason that you're asking that question?"

- *"That's a very good question.* Can you tell me more about why you asked it?"

- *"May I ask you a question?* Can you tell me where your question is coming from?"

- *"I'm glad you brought that up.* Is there a reason that you asked?"

Other Valuable Softening Statements

- *"I understand."*

- *"That's a very good point."*

- *"That's important."*

- *"Good question!"*

- *"You make an excellent point!"*

- *"Please help me understand your question better."*

- *"I agree."*

- *"No one has asked me that question in a long time."*

- *"I've been hearing that question a lot lately."*

PAIN Rule #6

The first problem that you hear from the customer is *never* the real problem.

Because buyers instinctively guard against reveal-ing their PAIN by protecting it in layers of insulation, they *never* show the real problem up front. Instead they give the salesperson their intellectual version of the problem, which is not the deepest PAIN, and therefore not the true buying motive.

This is an easy trap for salespeople to fall into be-cause they tend to believe the customer's initial assess-ment of his problem. When salespeople accept these sur-face statements at face value, they are effectively held at arm's length from discovering the real PAIN. The result is that salespeople unwittingly cooperate with the cus-tomer in his attempt to disguise his true buying motive, thereby significantly reducing their chance of finding the PAIN, solving the problem, and making the sale.

An Example

Imagine that you are a financial planner and a prospect calls and informs you that he has recently inher-ited $500,000, and that he wants to meet with you to dis-cuss how he might invest it.

In such a meeting, the vast majority of salespeople would mistakenly assume that this is the *only* problem to be solved, and the conversation would likely go something like this:

Prospect: "I don't know much about investing money. What do you recommend that I do?"

SP: "Plan A (blah, blah, blah), plan B (blah, blah, blah), or plan C (blah, blah, blah) are all good choices."

At this point the customer is intimidated and overwhelmed by all the information that the salesperson has presented, so much so that he feels too emotionally uncomfortable to make a decision. But he isn't about to reveal his discomfort to the salesperson for fear either of making a mistake, or of being perceived as "naive"—maybe even a little "stupid"—in terms of his ability to comprehend the information. As a result, he stalls for time by lying to the seller with a statement like,

Prospect: "I sure appreciate your help. This is a big
decision for me; I'll need to think it over,
discuss it with my wife, and then I'll get back
to you." (buyer's step three—TIO)

The point is that by treating the first problem presented by the customer as his real problem, the salesperson completely overlooked the fact that there is a deeper PAIN—in this case the buyer's emotional discomfort about making a decision too soon. Because of that oversight, the buyer defended himself with a white lie, and the salesperson immediately fell prey to the buyer's process—withholding information, stealing information, etc.—as discussed in Chapter 6. The way to prevent relinquishing such control to the buyer is to remember that the first problem he presents is never his real PAIN. The real PAIN lies deeper, and you must find it (see rule 7).

PAIN Rule #7

**Skillfully lead the customer away
from facts and toward his feelings.**

Almost always, what the buyer presents to the salesperson initially is intellectual, or factual, in nature. Often this is expressed in the form of a question, but not always. He may say statements like,

- "I'm interested in _____."

- "I'm looking for a _____."

- "I need a quote on _____."

Or, he could ask a product-related question like,

- "When can I expect delivery?"

- "What colors do they come in?"

- "Why should I buy your lift truck rather than your competitor's?"

Each of these statements or questions are *factual* in nature as opposed to being *emotional*, or *feeling*-oriented. However, PAIN is always emotional. In order to lead a buyer to his PAIN, therefore, you must skillfully move him from the facts that he presents up front into the realm of his feelings where his PAIN resides.

This transition—from fact to feeling—is precisely the purpose of reversing (rule 4). By turning a customer's statement or question around through asking another question, you lead him to discover the emotional source of his question or comment. Said another way, his factual verbalizations are merely *indicators* of his underlying PAIN; they are not the PAIN itself. Reversing helps greatly to move the discussion in the direction of uncovering that PAIN.

You will know that you have found the buyer's PAIN when you have reversed him to the point that he be-

153

gins to use "negative" *feeling* words to describe his situation. As a general rule, it takes three to five reverses before he reaches his actual PAIN, which he expresses in words like:

frustrated	worried	concerned
upset	afraid	uncomfortable
angry	anxious	burned out
irritated	scared	stressed

and similar words that express PAINful emotions.

All salespeople, though they don't often think in such terms, sell solutions that prevent or eliminate specific kinds of emotional PAIN. Dating services, for example, don't just match people or provide a social life for their members; they help reduce their clients' *fear* of meeting unsavory characters, or decrease their feelings of *loneliness* and *hopelessness*. Life insurance salespeople don't just sell policies to the interested consumer; they offer *peace of mind* to the *anxious* buyer who is *worried* about the security of his family in the event of his death.

Since nothing happens in business until something is sold, obviously sales are occurring at the surface level every day. Yet it is at this level—ordinary interest and everyday needs—that facts prevail; and price, which is *also* a fact, so easily becomes the primary focal point. But the truth is that the more a buyer *feels* his PAIN, the more eager and willing he is to get rid of it, and the less focused he is on price. Knowing this, you can begin to imagine the power a salesperson has when he masters the art of leading the customer away from his self-protective facts toward his PAINful feelings from where the facts emanated.

PAIN Rule #8

Ask open-ended questions.

Questions can be categorized into three basic types: closed, semi-open, and open. A closed question is one that elicits one-word responses, such as "yes," "no," or a factual answer. Examples would be "Are you ready for the meeting?" "Has business been good lately?" and "What time do you want to meet for lunch?" All are closed questions because they can be answered with a simple "yes," "no," or "twelve-fifteen."

A semi-open question is one that invites short-answer responses consisting of more than one word. Questions like "What did your supervisor say to do in his absence?" "When were you hoping to meet again?" and "What is the sales forecast for the next quarter?" elicit short answers like "Carry on as usual," "Sometime next week," and "We expect sales to increase by ten percent." Each semi-open question draws out slightly more information than a closed question is capable of getting, but not nearly enough to elicit all of a buyer's PAIN.

Open-ended questions are different, however, in that they are designed to stimulate complete thoughts and draw out lengthier responses from the customer. They are much more valuable than closed or semi-open questions for uncovering the buyer's PAIN because they invite the opportunity for him to reveal more information and lead you to his true buying motive.

For example, the question "What does the decision-making process look like in your company?" is likely to pull out much more information than "Do you make the decision?" (closed) or "Who makes the decision in situations like this?" (semi-open). Similarly, "What has been your experience with your current vacuum sweeper?" is a far superior question to "Are you happy with your current vacuum sweeper?" (closed) or "How is your current vacuum sweeper working for you?" (semi-open).

Clearly, there are appropriate times in the sales process to use closed and semi-open questions. However, for purposes of helping a customer discover his PAIN, open-ended questions are by far the most beneficial of the three, and should be used extensively in the sales interview, especially in the early stages.

Incidentally, suppose that you intended to ask an open-ended question but by mistake you asked a closed question instead. Don't panic; the question can be easily opened up again by waiting for the customer's response, and then asking a universal question (see PAIN rule 9). Actually, this "principle of easy recovery" is applicable to *all* of the techniques in Leadership Selling, so worrying about doing everything right all the time is unnecessary. The fact is that the more you practice the various techniques, the more naturally you will utilize other parts of the system to compensate for your errors.

PAIN Rule #9

Ask universal questions.

Some open-ended questions are generic enough to apply to almost any situation. That is, they are appropriate to ask regardless of what the customer has said. Examples of universal questions include:

- *"Can you tell me more about that?"* This has the appearance of a closed question in that the customer could conceivably answer "yes" or "no." In practice, however, this rarely happens, as people typically respond positively to your request by giving you additional information. You needn't fear a person answering with a yes or a no, however. In the rare instance that this might occur, simply ask the next question. If a person answers "yes," just say, "I'm glad—please continue"; if he answers "no," just say, "I can respect that" and then go on to the next question.

- *"Please help me understand that better."* As with some of the other universal questions, this is not technically a question, although it functions as one in that its purpose is to keep the customer talking (rule 1).

- *"You must be asking (or telling) me that for a reason."*

- *"Can you be more specific?"*

- *"Please talk to me about that."*

- *"Which means?"*

- *"Please say more."*

We strongly recommend that you memorize these seven universal questions, as doing so will help you master Leadership Selling in the most efficient way possible.

The reason is that one of the first stumbling blocks salespeople face is knowing that they should ask a question but they can't think of an appropriate question to ask at that specific moment. When this happens, salespeople tend to lapse back into old habits by presenting features, advantages, and benefits. To avoid this costly mistake, one can immediately retrieve a universal question from his memory, which accomplishes two important objectives. First, it keeps the conversation moving from fact to feeling (rule 7); second, it buys you time to formulate your next question.

PAIN Rule #10

Ask key-off questions.

In recent years there has been a slight shift in emphasis for salespeople to present less and qualify more by probing and asking relevant questions. Various selling systems stress the use of this approach. The problem with these systems is that many of their questions are predetermined—that is, they are scripted and memorized in advance of the actual sales call. A few examples include:

"Do you use X?"

"How many Xs do you use per week?"

"Who is your current supplier?"

"Are you looking to purchase additional Xs in the

near future?"

"Who makes the decision on purchasing Xs?"

Notice that each of these questions are either closed or semi-open. They seek facts—hard data—rather than underlying feelings. Yet it is only in his feelings that the buyer's PAIN, or real buying motive, can be found.

Every piece of factual information that a customer relinquishes, whether intentional or not, has emotional significance. Consequently, it is much better that your questions "key-off" his replies rather than rely on predetermined questions that may or may not relate to the information that he gives you.

Suppose, for instance, that you sell real estate and you ask the prospective buyer, "What type of house are you looking for?" Suppose he answers, "A two-story home with four bedrooms." It would be far better to key-off this information with a question that relates directly to his reply, rather than ask your next canned question. That is, instead of asking next, "What location are you looking for?"—which is semi-open, factual in nature, and unrelated to the buyer's previous response, key-off what was actually said. This is why the universal questions are so valuable, because they can be used easily to key-off information from almost any response that is given.

Again, when the prospect says, "A two-story home with four bedrooms," ask a universal question such as:

"Can you tell me more about that?" or

"Please tell me more about why two stories, or why four bedrooms?" or

"You must be telling me two stories and four bedrooms for a reason...."

There is a reason, of course, or the person wouldn't be giving you that information. Perhaps he has a large family and needs that many bedrooms; maybe he works out of his home and plans to convert one or more of the bedrooms into office space; maybe he has no children but entertains overnight guests frequently. The point is that in any of these scenarios, it would be PAINful to *not* have four bedrooms, and remember, people buy to prevent or relieve their PAIN. By keying-off whatever factual information a buyer gives you, it is possible to lead him to his PAIN in a direct and efficient manner.

PAIN Rule #11

Ask vertical questions.

To understand the full meaning of vertical questioning, consider this analogy. Two cities in Texas, Midland and Odessa, are settlements where the sagebrush grows and tumbleweeds blow across the land. No one could have imagined in days of old that directly beneath the surface were rich pockets of oil just waiting to be discovered.

The way that tumbleweeds travel across the fields at Midland and Odessa could be compared to the way questions are asked in traditional sales. We refer to this method as "horizontal" questioning because, even though the questions are often predetermined or scripted in advance, they fail to penetrate the surface, or "factual zone."

Just as tumbleweeds blow across the surface of the land over the valuable oil below, so it is with salespeople who use horizontal questions. They accept fact after fact from the customer without regard to the PAIN that lies beneath his remarks. Vertical questions, on the other hand, can be likened to an oil-drilling rig, which is designed to deliberately work its way through the surface rock to reach the "black gold" that lies beneath. Like the drill, salespeople who use vertical questions move purposely into the well-guarded "emotional zone" of the customer where his PAIN is hidden.

The following scenarios illustrate how vertical questions differ from horizontal questions in terms of digging deeper into three specific comments that a salesperson might hear from a customer:

Customer: *"I need at least five hundred dots per inch from a printer."*

Traditional Salesperson (using a horizontal question):
            "No problem. How soon do you need it?"

Leadership Salesperson (using a **vertical** question):
            "Can you help me understand why you say 'at least five hundred dots per inch'?"

*****

Customer: *"How much is this equipment?"*

Traditional Salesperson (using a horizontal question):
            "It's five hundred nineteen dollars and ninety-five cents. How would you like to pay—cash, check, or charge?"

Leadership Salesperson (using a **vertical** question): *"I know that's an important question, but there are several variables involved in order to answer it. **May I ask exactly how you were planning to use it and what you hope to accomplish?**"*

*****

Customer: *"We need to develop a policy manual."*

Traditional Salesperson (using a horizontal question): *"How many pages will it have?"*

Leadership Salesperson (using a **vertical** question): *"That sounds important. **Can you tell me more about your need for a policy manual?**"*

In each of these examples, the vertical question is designed to penetrate into the next emotional layer of the customer's remark rather than stay at the surface, or factual, level. Each question probes *into* the PAIN like the oil-drilling rig rather than *passing over the top* of it like the tumbleweeds.

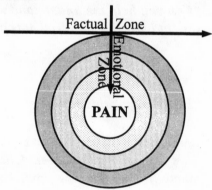

Figure 11

PAIN Rule #12

Ask, and then be silent while you wait for the reply.

As a general rule, people are uncomfortable with silence when it occurs in a conversation. Yet when you ask a buyer a question that purposely elicits PAINful information from him, he often pauses in silence to reflect on his answer. Since he is not used to thinking about his PAIN, his answer is not likely to be instantly available to him as if it were already on the tip of his tongue. He needs to reflect quietly for a moment, and it is extremely important that you allow him to do so without interruption.

At first this can be a difficult assignment for salespeople who are more accustomed to talking rather than asking and listening. In addition, some salespeople become uncomfortable themselves when they see their customer on the edge of feeling PAIN, especially if their questions are directly responsible for bringing it to the surface.

To their detriment, many salespeople fill the void of silence by talking, which in effect *rescues* the customer from feeling his PAIN rather than *leading* him to it. While this is an understandable reaction, it is absolutely counterproductive to their primary objective of getting the buyer to admit his PAIN (rule 13).

If this applies to you, we recommend that you practice getting comfortable with silence. You might practice outside of your work environment where you don't feel pressured to make a sale. Ask a question, and then be quiet and listen until the other person answers. With practice, you will be surprised that your comfort level with silence will increase. Remember, your customer's silence is where he discovers his PAIN, which is precisely why you must listen with intense concentration.

PAIN Rule #13

Your customer must admit his PAIN.

By "admit" his PAIN we mean that it is important that your prospect actually verbalizes his PAIN rather than you saying the words for him. When you state his PAIN, he doesn't necessarily believe it; when he says it, he does. It would be much more effective, for instance, for the *buyer* to say,

> "I am worried about what will happen if I don't buy (whatever you sell),"

than for *you* to say,

> "You will be worried about what will happen if you don't buy (whatever I sell)."

First of all, the prospect could easily disagree with you, thereby in effect denying his PAIN. But even if he agrees with you, it won't bring him to the same level of awareness of his PAIN as when he actually says the words himself.

The goal, remember, is to help the customer discover—and *admit*—his PAIN. Assuming that you have a solution, it is when he is actually *feeling* his PAIN that he is most ready to buy a solution. This is because in his heightened awareness of his emotional discomfort, he is motivated to do whatever is necessary to eliminate it.

PAIN Rule #14

"Actively" listen to your customer.

Few people would argue with the statement that the vast majority of people are not especially skilled at listening, albeit for a variety of reasons. When we are engaged in a conversation with someone, we are often more focused on what we are going to say next than on what the other person may be saying at the moment. In some cases, the problem is that we are so disengaged from the conversation that our mind wanders to thoughts unrelated to the subject at hand, which makes it impossible to listen intently.

Yet listening may be one of the most important skills that a salesperson must have, *especially* those who are committed to mastering Leadership Selling. The simple truth is that it is *impossible* to help your customers discover their PAIN unless you become proficient at listening. It is your ability to listen well that:

- demonstrates to your customer your empathy and concern for his situation;

- supplies you with important information to formulate your next key-off question (rule 10);

- enables you to recognize the real PAIN when it

is actually expressed.

Skillful listening could easily be discussed in an entire book by itself, and in fact, there are several good books available on this subject. However, our goal here is to merely introduce you to the basic principles of "active" listening in order to get you acquainted with some of the fundamental techniques.

~

The three fundamental skills of active listening are parroting, paraphrasing, and feeling feedback. There is purpose in listing them in this specific sequence, because they are increasingly challenging to execute, just as they are increasingly more effective at letting your customer know that you really do hear him. A helpful tip to follow is that you become the best listener when you use a balanced mixture of all three skills rather than overuse any one of them.

Parroting

As an active listening skill, parroting is just what the name implies, namely, repeating exactly what a customer says back to him just as a parrot would do. Unlike the parrot, however, you must change the pronouns when you use this technique. For example:

Buyer: "I'm looking for your product in blue."

SP: "(So) you're looking for my product in blue."

If the sentence is too long and cumbersome to repeat, simply parrot back the key words, which are usually the last words spoken.

Buyer: "I've always bought a blue car since I learned how to drive, and I don't think I'll ever buy a different color."

SP: "(It sounds like) you don't think you'll ever buy a different color."

While it is important to use a mixture of active listening skills as mentioned, try to avoid parroting more than twice in a row, as this can become annoying to your customers.

Paraphrasing

The objective when you paraphrase is to use different words to reiterate what your customer says without changing its meaning.

Buyer: "I need a car that gets good gas mileage."

SP: "(So) fuel economy is important to you."

*****

Buyer: "I'd like to know who else you've done business with before I make a decision."

SP: "It sounds like you'd like some references before proceeding."

By saying back to the customer what he means without using his exact words, you have in essence said to him, "I hear what you're saying, and I understand."

Feeling Feedback

The most advanced of the three basic active listening skills, feeling feedback is especially valuable for hearing and acknowledging a customer's PAIN. Remember, since people *feel* PAIN, it will be expressed in *feeling*-type words. When you detect a customer using a feeling word that expresses discomfort, repeat the feeling back to him. To do so (1) acknowledges that you heard him correctly, (2) allows him to either confirm or, if necessary, fine-tune his explanation of what he is feeling, and (3) magnifies his awareness of his own PAIN, thereby allowing him to see it more clearly.

Buyer: "I need to be certain that this software program has the versatility to adapt to the changing needs of our growing business."

SP: "(It sounds like) you're *worried* that the demands of your business might outgrow the capabilities of the system prematurely."

Notice that this statement *acknowledges* the buyer's feeling, *feeds it back to him* for confirmation or further explanation, and *magnifies* his awareness of his PAIN.

Sometimes salespeople express concern that they will misinterpret the buyer's feeling and feed it back to him incorrectly. Upon closer examination, however, it becomes clear that there is nothing to really worry about. Only one of two outcomes is possible, and both of them position you to penetrate further into his PAIN.

If you send his feeling back correctly, he will confirm it, which of course is what you want. If you don't, he will say so, in which case you are in the perfect position to say, "I'm sorry (struggle), please help me understand better what you do feel" (a universal question). In both cases, you are working systematically to help him discover his underlying PAIN.

Also, watch your customer for signals as to whether or not you are listening effectively. A smile, a nod of the head, a simple "yes," statements like "Exactly!" or "You're right"—these are clear expressions from him that you understand his *feelings*. He is, in effect, thanking you for listening and hearing him correctly, while at the same time giving you implicit permission to continue with your questions.

Before leaving the discussion on active listening, one last suggestion that will greatly enhance your listening skills is to take notes during the conversation with each and every customer. Doing so accomplishes three important objectives: (1) you must listen closely in order to record important points that he makes; (2) it makes him aware that he has your full attention and that you think what he has to say is important; and (3) it furnishes a written record for future reference as to what your customer actually said, which at a later date reinforces his perception that you did in fact hear him.

PAIN Rule #15

PAIN is personal.

Since "one man's meat is another man's poison," never assume that two people have the same PAIN in the

169

same situation; and even if they do, that they experience the same PAIN identically. One customer could ask, "What accessories are available for X?" because he needs a specific type and will purchase it if one is available. However, another customer could ask exactly the same question, yet have an entirely different motive, such as wanting information that he can use to shop around.

We have all heard that we should never "assume" because it is a source of communication breakdown and creates much misunderstanding. No place is this more true than as it relates to helping people discover their PAIN. PAIN is always personal in that it is unique to the perception of each individual. Even when two people feel exactly the same PAIN—stress, for example—they are likely to manifest their PAIN differently. Stress to one individual may be experienced as stomach pains, yet another person under the same stress may experience sleeplessness. The point is, never assume that you know what a person's PAIN is until you lead him to his PAIN and he verbalizes it. To do otherwise is to miss a valuable selling opportunity.

Also, for salespeople whose sales cycle requires calling on more than one individual in the same company, it is especially important to keep this principle in mind. You may call on Mike, the account manager, and do a wonderful job of finding his PAIN. However, when Mike passes you on to David, the project manager, you can be certain that David's PAIN is personal and unique to him. Therefore, make sure that you start over by helping David verbalize his *own* PAIN rather than assume that he shares Mike's PAIN. Many a sale has been lost as a result of not observing this very important rule.

PAIN Rule #16

Know when to stop searching for PAIN.

Salespeople often ask us how they can know when they have found their prospect's real PAIN, and therefore when to stop asking PAIN-related questions. The answer is, when you hear your customer speaking in "negative" feeling words, such as worried, frustrated, stressed, and so on.

It would be senseless to ask questions beyond this point. Once a person tells you that he is "afraid of losing his job unless he purchases X," you might want to go one more step and ask something like, "And that would mean what to you?" If he responds, "I would lose my home and family," it would be inappropriate to ask, "Can you tell me more about that?" Such depth of questioning is the proper function of psychotherapy, but has no place in sales.

The bottom line is that you only lead a buyer to the level of PAIN that relates directly to whatever product or service you sell, and no further. But while it is important to understand these limits, the reality of the situation is that you must be much more concerned about getting *enough* PAIN rather than *too much* PAIN. If salespeople make one mistake more consistently than any other while learning to perfect Leadership Selling, it is to stop too early in the questioning process. They mistakenly believe that they've found *the* PAIN when all they have really found are surface facts that indicate the likelihood that PAIN lies deeper.

PAIN Rule #17

Ask the tough questions.

Salespeople are notorious for avoiding questions that might upset their customer in some way. *Yet in order to perform Leadership Selling effectively, you must ask the tough questions!*

For example, let's suppose that your job includes collecting money from a customer whose payment is delinquent. You have a good relationship with him that you don't want to jeopardize. Rather than ignore or postpone confronting the problem, it is imperative that you ask the tough questions in order to resolve the problem.

But you don't have to phrase it as directly as, "Are you going to pay your bill?" "Tough" doesn't automatically mean "blunt." This is where the other Leadership Selling skills come into play. They become interlocking pieces of a puzzle which together form a highly effective selling system.

The concept of struggling to keep your customer OK, for example, can be very effective for softening tough questions:

> *"Bob, this is really difficult for me to do, and I need your help. The credit department is on my case to ask you about your late payment, and although I know you're good for the money, I don't know what to tell them. Can you help me out?"*

Actually, there's a valuable technique in operation here that has widespread application when asking the tough questions. This strategy is sometimes referred to as the "good guy, bad guy" approach. Essentially, you create a triangle where you are one point of the triangle, your customer is a second point, and an appropriate third party is the third point. In the example with Bob, the third point of the triangle was the credit department.

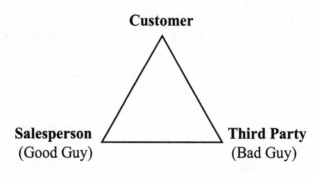

Customer

Salesperson
(Good Guy)

Third Party
(Bad Guy)

Figure 12

The goal is for you to be the good guy so that you can stay bonded with your customer, and let the third party be the bad guy who takes the blame. All you need to do is to ask the tough question on behalf of the bad guy, and then ask for help in satisfying the third party. This is a very effective technique for asking the tough questions, and it works well in many other circumstances, as well.

PAIN Rule #18

Keep the ball on the other side of the court.

Using the game of tennis as an analogy, the goal in Leadership Selling is to keep the action on the other side of the net where your customer is playing. That is, keep the responsibility for answering the questions in his court rather than in your court. This relates, of course, to keeping your customer talking (rule 1) and the whole concept of reversing (rule 4).

It is important to understand, however, that reversing is a much broader concept than simply *answering* a question with another question. Reversing is *any* technique that you might use to keep your customer talking and giving you important information, instead of you talking and giving valuable information to him. Many of these techniques have already been covered, such as active listening, open-ended questions, and so on. Others include:

- **Answer and Then Ask.** If a customer asks you a technical question, which now you know is an intellectualization of his PAIN, you might answer his question briefly and then ask about the *reason* that he is inquiring. For instance, if you were asked,

  Buyer: "How many revolutions per minute does this machine make?"

  you might answer,

  SP: "Six thousand—(your answer) but for what reason do you ask?" (your question)

Note that we deliberately did not suggest that you ask the question "why?" because it tends to put people on the defensive, which interferes with the bonding process. The word "why" should be avoided at all costs, therefore, and "for what reason?" should be substituted in its place. While buyers can be offended when asked "why?" they are usually quite willing to tell you their *reason* for asking.

- **Give an Incomplete Answer, Pause, and Then Ask.**

  Buyer: "How many languages are your textbooks printed in?"

  SP: "Hey, that's a good question. Uh, six or seven (pause)...but can you tell me the reason that you asked?"

- **One or Two Word Prompters.** Often you can keep a person talking simply by saying one or two words that serve as a green light for him to continue. For example,

  Buyer: "I'm thinking of making some changes around here."

  SP: "Such as..."

Other common prompters include "And...," "So...," "Because...," "Therefore...," "But...," and "Meaning...." In every instance, the purpose for using them is to get the ball on the customer's side of the court and keep him talking.

PAIN Rule #19

Get to "no" as fast as you can!

Salespeople are forever working to get their customers to say "yes." Customers typically experience this as pressure, and it is only natural for them to resist. A big part of their resistance is to withhold information, especially anything that might be related to their PAIN. Since it is your customer's PAIN that is the "object of your hunt," so to speak, it is imperative that you remove any obstacles that might interfere with your search.

One such obstacle is your customer's reluctance to tell you "no" for fear of hurting your feelings. Most people would rather be polite by telling white lies to salespeople—"I need to talk to my manager," "I'd like to think it over," etc.—than to openly reject them. Such deception on the customer's part, even though well-intentioned, hinders your attempts to draw out his PAIN.

As mentioned in Chapter 14, to ensure that customers are more honest with you, tell them early in the interview that it's okay to say "no." The problem is that while this may put the buyer at ease, it can cause tremendous discomfort for a salesperson until he masters the technique. Giving the customer permission to say no seems to a salesperson to be in direct violation of what he has always believed he was supposed to do. The irony is that the more one tries to get a customer to tell him "no," the less likely it will happen. But these will just be empty words until you try this technique yourself to see that it truly does work.

When you put the customer at ease so that he can feel comfortable telling you "no," not only is he *less* likely to give you bogus objections, he is *more* likely to be open and honest, and reveal his true PAIN.

In addition to making it safe for him to say no, it is also important to try to get him to say no as fast as possible. The sooner you do this, the faster you will be able to determine whether he is a "suspect" or a "prospect." A suspect who feels at ease will likely be direct and tell you "no" rather than lie to you in order to be polite; a prospect won't tell a lie *or* say "no" because he is interested in seeking a solution to his PAIN.

The Concept of "Negative" Reverse

There are a number of strategies for trying to get your customer to say "no," most of which fall under the category of a "negative" reverse—that is, a reverse with the word "no" built into it: won't, don't, wouldn't, couldn't, and so on. For example, if you said to a customer, "You probably *wouldn't* want to see our newest product," he is far more likely to say, "Yes, I would" than "No, I wouldn't." Even though you are phrasing it in a way that makes it perfectly okay for him to say no, it is difficult for him to do so.

Outside of the field of sales, this is sometimes referred to as "reverse psychology." Many readers will know that this is a highly effective method for getting people to act in a certain way. Again, that's the paradox of the situation. The more you try to get customers to say "no," the less they will actually say it.

To continue with the previous example, you have just said to your customer, "You *probably wouldn't* want to see our newest product...," and he says, "Yes, I would." It is important to understand that you would *not* immediately present simply because he asked you to. Remember, there is an underlying PAIN as to *why* he wants to see it. Therefore, when he says, "Yes, I would," you must ask another question to keep working to discover his real PAIN, such as, "Is there something you were hoping for in particular?" or "Can you tell me more about your reason for being interested?" or "It *wouldn't* be a waste of your time, would it?" (another negative reverse).

If at this point he responds in vague terms, such as "It depends," continue to work toward his PAIN. Ask,

"Which means...?" and so on until he reveals his PAIN.

Some salespeople worry that their customers will experience negative reverses as being blunt or abrasive. The secret to keeping them from being perceived in this way is to make sure that you say them gently. It is common knowledge that the *way* you say something conveys more meaning than the actual words that you use.

Negative reverses have such diverse application across a wide range of situations that it would be impossible to list them all here. The list would be endless. Examples, however, would include statements like:

- *"I don't suppose you're ready to make a decision on this yet."*

- *"You probably wouldn't want to get together to discuss this."*

- *"There's probably nothing that would cause you to consider another supplier."*

- *"I don't suppose you could decide this without talking to someone else."*

- *"Your boss probably isn't in today, is he?"*

Another type of negative reverse is making statements in the extreme. Most people will deny the truth of extreme statements, which has the effect of moving them in the opposite direction, closer to their PAIN. Examples would include:

- *"You're probably too busy to talk with me."*

- *"Your business is probably going too well to look at any alternatives."*

- *"You're probably totally happy with your current supplier."*

PAIN Rule #20

Frame your questions in hypothetical language.

PAIN is always difficult to admit, since admitting to it is the equivalent of having to feel it. An effective method you can use to get customers to discover their own PAIN is to make it seem less "real" by encouraging them to talk about it in hypothetical language. It is inherently safer for a person to respond to a question like, "*Let's pretend* there's one thing you could have done better on your last project; what might it be?" than to the real question, "What could you have done better on the last project?"

The difference lies in the fact that whatever one says in response to the hypothetical question can be rescinded, which is not as true with the real-life question. This difference, slight as it might seem, is a powerful tool for helping customers to discover their PAIN because, in the end, they can always deny the truth of what they said. Nevertheless, whatever they say while speaking in the hypothetical is more than likely indicative of the real PAIN.

Jon, for example, is the personnel director at a large manufacturing company. Bob, who represents a firm that sells liability insurance to corporations, calls on Jon in the hope of selling him a new liability package. If Bob were to say to Jon, "What are the limitations of your current coverage?" Jon might well say, "We're pretty happy with it, actually." However, suppose Bob were to ask, "*Let's imagine* that you could improve your current liability coverage in some way—what would that look like?" Now Bob is far more likely to get an honest answer because he has posed the situation in a hypothetical framework, which is nonthreatening.

In general, hypothetical questions begin with the following types of words:

- "If...?"

- "What if...?"

- "Let's pretend that..."

- "Let's say that..."

- "Suppose you could..."

- "Assuming that..."

- "Let's imagine that..."

It is best to utilize a mixture of hypothetical questions with your customer so as not to overuse any one particular phrase. Actually, because of the subtle power inherent in the language of Leadership Selling, a good rule to follow is—*never overuse any specific phrase with a customer, since doing so allows that which is intended to be subtle to become more obvious, thereby detracting from its power.*

PAIN Rule #21

Get the problem on the table.

When a salesperson fears something in relation to an interaction with a customer, it is best to state his fear early in the sales call. For instance, let's say a salesperson is afraid that his customer won't purchase from him unless he offers a discount. Since his company refuses to discount their products, it would be best for him to say, "My company doesn't offer discounts, and I'm concerned that you won't purchase my product because of that. Is that true?"

Usually the customer will say something like "No, not necessarily," in which case you should say, "Which means?" thus beginning the descent into his PAIN. If by chance he does say, "You're quite right—I wouldn't be interested without a discount," the salesperson should respond with something to the effect of, "I understand. So there's probably no reason for us to keep talking—is that true?" (a negative reverse). If the prospect says "yes" to this, in effect it is a "no," which is the second best answer you could hear.

Remember, "maybe's" and "let me think it over's" must not be tolerated in Leadership Selling. The reason, again, is that when you accept them, you are mostly wasting your time. They are used by the customer to forestall having to make a commitment, or to dismiss you altogether. Your job is to convert "maybe's" and "let me think it over's" either into commitments to move forward, or into outright "no's."

In effect, putting the problem on the table precludes your customer from using it to his advantage at a later point by saying such things as "maybe" or "let me think it over." By bringing the problem up early, you have blocked any attempt that he might use later to stall in order to deflect your efforts to discover his PAIN.

PAIN Rule #22

Call the game.

Another way of saying this is to "state the obvious" in situations where something is happening between you and your customer that could conceivably interfere with your search for his PAIN. If he appears angry, say, "You seem angry"; if he appears to be in a hurry, then say, "It looks like you're in a hurry"; if he acts disinterested in what you have to say, then say, "You seem disinterested in what I have to say."

By stating the obvious, you neutralize the game that your customer is playing, even if he is playing it unconsciously. Whenever a buyer's game loses its power, you have removed another major obstacle that he might have otherwise used against you to block you from finding his PAIN.

The twenty-two preceding PAIN rules, when used in combination, form the very core of Leadership Selling. The remainder of the system revolves around one's ability to learn, internalize, and apply these rules. They are not isolated rules; rather, they should be viewed as interlocking links in a chain. But a chain is only as strong as its weakest link. Similarly, your ability to help your customer find his PAIN is only as strong as your mastery of *all* twenty-two rules, not just those that come naturally or are initially the easiest for you to apply.

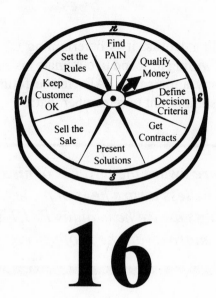

16

Qualifying for Money

Qualifying for money in Leadership Selling is a significantly different process than it is in most other sales methodologies. To most salespeople, it means trying to determine whether the customer can afford what they sell. In Leadership Selling, however:

> **Qualifying for money is the equivalent of *quantifying* the buyer's PAIN in terms of dollars.**

In other words, it is determining the amount of money he is willing to spend to eliminate his current PAIN or prevent any anticipated PAIN in the future. Toward this end, it is important to remember that:

> *The **more** aware the buyer is of his PAIN,*
> *the **less** aware he is of price;*
> *the **less** aware he is of his PAIN, the*
> ***more** aware he is of price.*

There are untold numbers of salespeople who believe that they can't compete effectively "when the other guy's price is lower." But the real problem is that they have yet to realize the important correlation between the buyer's *awareness* of his PAIN and the price issue. Consequently, they unknowingly allow the consumer to focus on price, thereby making it a much larger issue than it really is.

The point is that qualifying prospects for money is a much easier job than is commonly thought *as long as* you find the customer's PAIN *before* discussing the price issue. If, however, the customer asks about the price early on, as often happens, you simply keep him OK by saying:

> *"I know that's an important question, and I understand that you'll have to be comfortable with the price. Before I can give you an accurate answer, however, I'm going to need some information from you—would that be okay?"*

In this way, you have effectively reversed his question and

have started to lead the buyer away from *his* search for price to *your* search for PAIN.

Another common problem related to qualifying customers for money is the salesperson's own comfort level in relation to money. Dale is a salesperson who recently shared the following story with us:

It was the holiday season and I was shopping in the jewelry section of a department store for a Christmas present for my wife. While I was looking, a middle-aged gentleman came in and asked to see ladies' wristwatches. The salesclerk responded by pulling out a display of watches from the glass case ranging in price from $19.95 to $39.95. Before the gentleman could say anything, the clerk suggested to him that the best buy was the watch priced at $24.95 that had been marked down from $39.95.

Politely, the man thanked the clerk for showing him the watches and walked away. I was browsing and taking my time, and after a few minutes the same man reappeared and purposely sought out a different clerk. I heard him say to her quietly, "Do you have any 'good' watches?" Appropriately, the salesperson asked the customer what he had in mind, and he responded, "Something over five hundred dollars." The clerk assured him that she did, and invited him to follow her to the proper display case.

"Wow," I thought to myself, "what a lesson about different salespeople's comfort level with money!"

The moral of the story is that the first salesperson's comfort level with money skewed her entire perception of the customer's request. Because her comfort level was closer to the lower range of prices than to the higher-priced watches, she mistakenly selected the inexpensive watches, assuming that they were what he wanted to see. Even if the gentleman had asked the first clerk to see watches "over five hundred dollars," she more than likely would have tried to steer him to the less expensive watches because that is the dollar amount with which she was the most comfortable.

This particular problem of one's own comfort level with money plagues many a salesperson with regard to qualifying the customer about money. Because she would never spend $500 for a wristwatch herself, she projected her own financial comfort zone into the customer's monetary intentions.

In Leadership Selling, a salesperson must ensure that he is comfortable with the entire spectrum of prices that he charges to prevent the above scenario from occurring. As part of this, he must suspend *all* expectations and *all* judgments about the buyer's interests or intentions, and systematically qualify him for his PAIN, including quantifying the amount of money he is willing to spend to alleviate it.

Failure to properly qualify one's customers for money has long been a nemesis for people in the selling profession. Many brilliant "dog and pony" shows performed by sellers have ended in disappointment when the prospective customer says, "I agree that it's a great product, but I'm afraid it's way out of my price range." For this reason:

> *Money issues must be addressed **before** giving a presentation, just as PAIN-related issues must be discussed before talking about money.*

By doing so, you save enormous amounts of time because you flush out the so-called "tire kickers" early, thereby separating the suspects from the prospects.

Applying PAIN Rules to Qualifying for Money

Situation One

When you know that the other guy's price is lower *before* the sales call, then get the problem on the table (rule 21) and get to "no" as fast as you can (rule 19). For example:

> *"My company is not the least expensive provider out there—is that going to be a problem?"* (rule 21)

or

> *"Our product is one of the more expensive ones around—is that reason for us to stop talking?"* (rule 21)

or

> *"Our product is the most expensive of its kind. So you probably wouldn't be interested after knowing that, would you...."* (rule 19)

If the buyer responds that he wants to continue the conversation, then begin to ask PAIN-related questions, such as:

> *"Really? Why would that be?"* (rule 8)

If he indicates, however, that he does not want to continue, you can say something like:

> *"Please talk to me about that."* (rule 9)

*****

Situation Two

When you *don't* know in advance of the sales call whether the other guy's price is lower, or, for that matter, if they are even looking at "another guy," your goal is to ascertain your prospect's budget to quantify his PAIN in terms of dollars. You might say, for example:

> *"The good news is that I can probably help you solve your problem. The bad news is that it may cost more than what you anticipated."*

Invariably, the customer will respond with the question, "How much will it cost?" Your next move depends on which of two scenarios you are in. Either (a) your price is fixed and there is no room to negotiate, or (b) the price is entirely negotiable, depending on the details of the transaction.

(a) Fixed Price. When the customer asks, "How much will this cost?" you must state the price. Having done so, the next words out of your mouth are crucial to effectively qualify for money. Using language that is comfortable to you, you must say the equivalent of:

"Shall we stop?"

> or

"Is it over?"

> or

"Is there reason to keep talking?"

This is another version of getting the problem on the table and going for "no," and it is only said *after* you have already determined the buyer's PAIN.

(b) Negotiable Price. Again, when the customer asks, "How much will this cost?" your best response is to inflate the estimate by giving him a range. We recommend 10 percent to 20 percent over the price at which you're willing to sell, so that you leave ample room to negotiate. Since part of your customer's PAIN may be the cost itself, it helps him to lessen his PAIN about money to be able to negotiate for a lower price than you first quoted. For instance, if you are selling an item that costs in the vicinity of $300, you might say in response to his "how much?" question:

> *"I'm not sure until we talk further about the details of what you're looking for, but possibly as much as three hundred thirty to three sixty."*

As in scenario **(a)**, the next question that you ask is critical—*"Shall we stop?" "Is it over?" or "Is there reason to keep talking?"*

The entire process as just discussed in scenario **(b)** must occur in the place of what salespeople otherwise do, namely, answer the customer's "how much?" question directly. The process summarized is:

- qualify the customer by quantifying his PAIN in slightly-inflated round numbers,

- negotiate to determine his comfort level, and then

- propose an actual figure.

While this strategy is applicable to nearly every sales situation, it has particular relevance for any salesperson whose business involves submitting bids, quotes, and/or formal written proposals. The reason that it works well in these circumstances is because it eliminates untold hours of preparation that could easily have ended in no sale due to price.

Properly qualifying for money is an essential step to ensure that the customer cannot revert to using the price issue against you. Again, many of his price concerns wane once you've helped him discover his PAIN *before* discussing how much money he is willing to pay (to get rid of that PAIN). The truth is that failure to determine your customer's PAIN before attempting to qualify for money inadvertently sabotages any opportunity you might have had to *quantify* his PAIN, a step that is absolutely essential for exceptional selling "when the other guy's price is lower."

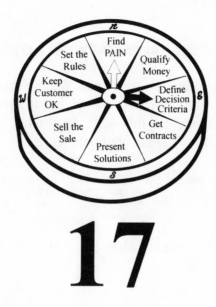

17

The Decision Step

If there is anything more frustrating for a salesper-son than giving a thorough presentation to an unqualified prospect, it is presenting to someone whom he assumes is the decision maker when in fact he is not. Countless hours are wasted day after day by many salespeople who do pre-cisely this. Not only is it disappointing and frustrating in addition to being a waste of time, it is also counterproduc-tive, demoralizing, and exhausting. For these reasons, salespeople who adopt the principles of Leadership Selling must follow a particular process in the decision step.

The Traditional Way of Finding the Decision Maker

Most selling systems acknowledge the importance of identifying the decision maker, but the methods they employ to accomplish this often don't work. Such questions as the following are commonplace:

"Who makes the decision to buy or not to buy?"

or

"Who besides you will be a part of making this decision?"

or

"Who do you consult with before making a final decision?"

These questions fall short in two significant ways. First, they are limited in that they are semi-open and elicit short responses from the customer, where the goal is to ask open-ended questions to get as much information as possible. Second, they subtly undermine your efforts to keep the customer OK because they implicitly attack his self-worth. That is, by asking a person a question that suggests that someone other than himself is involved in making the decision is to imply that he doesn't have the power to make the decision alone, which is very unempowering for—if not degrading of—that individual.

The Leadership Selling Way

Rather than focus on *who* the decision maker is, as the previous questions attempted to determine, it is important instead to:

> ## Focus on the *process* by which the decision is made.

To discover the decision-making process, one must ask open-ended questions like:

> *"What does the decision-making process look like in your company in regard to buying X?"*
>
> *"How do you go about making decisions in situations like this?"*
>
> *"How are decisions to buy X usually made around here?"*

When the *process* is fully disclosed, it will reveal either the actual decision maker or the person who represents him in his absence. Before we discuss the details of how to sell to the absentee decision maker, however, we can't emphasize enough that *a salesperson must never truly believe it when he is told that it is not possible to speak directly with the decision maker.* When he does automatically believe it, he thereby surrenders any real opportunity that he might have had to meet with him. Usually such a statement is given with the intention of protecting the decision maker's time. It may well be a company's policy that salespeople cannot talk with the decision maker, but this does not mean that the policy is cast in stone and that there can never be an exception to it.

The point is that you must be creative in your efforts—and, if necessary, be willing to persevere—to get to the decision maker. As the old adage goes, "If there's a will, there's a way." For example, would the decision maker turn down a conversation with the CEO of your company or with the VP of Sales and Marketing? Is it within your control to request that such a meeting be arranged?

The bottom line is that if you *don't* get to the decision maker, the chances that your product or service will be treated as a commodity—that is, that the decision will ultimately be based on price—are many times greater than if you do meet with him. Therefore, be willing to challenge—in a respectful manner, of course—any statement that suggests you cannot meet with the decision maker instead of simply accepting it as an indisputable fact.

On the assumption that you have done whatever it takes to meet with the decision maker, you have only one job to do—find his PAIN! No PAIN, no sale; it's as simple as that. Since you are now with the person that you ideally want to meet with, help him discover his PAIN as the prerequisite for determining whether or not you can sell him a solution.

Selling to the Absentee Decision Maker

Be advised, however, that even after you make a concerted effort to meet with the decision maker, there are still isolated situations when it will be impossible to do so. In such times, there are clear steps that you must follow to decrease your chances of being treated like a commodity—that is, as just another salesperson—yourself.

You must start by assuming that the person who is standing in the stead of the decision maker is, to one degree or another, an "influencer." That is, assume that he has the power to influence the actual decision maker in some way. While such individuals can't make the ultimate decision of saying "yes," they do have authority to say "no" by declining to meet with you, by refusing to pass the information up the ladder, and so on. You must therefore assume that every person is a decision maker to one degree or another.

With these factors in mind:

1. Determine if the influencer is your ally or your adversary. You can do this with questions like:

   "Suppose this decision were totally up to you, what would you do?"

   or

   "What do you think the decision should be?"

2. If his answer is negative, assume that he's an adversary, and continue just as you would if he were the actual decision maker. Try to discover his PAIN by asking him about his own reservations about purchasing your product in an effort to turn him into an ally.

   If on the other hand his answer is positive, then challenge him by asking:

   "For what reasons would you choose to work with me?"

   Remember, it can be very difficult for a person to actually say, "If it were up to me to decide, I wouldn't buy from you." Unless his self-esteem is unusually high, it is more comfortable for him to tell a white lie by responding, "Sure, I'd buy from you," and then later blame the decision *not* to buy on the actual decision maker. So you must question him to determine if his reasons for saying that he would buy from you are sincere. If there isn't good reason to change, people won't change. The rule of thumb always is, *no PAIN, no sale.* Therefore, your best test of his sincerity is the degree of his PAIN that you are able to uncover.

3. On the assumption that you have determined that he is a true ally, your next step is to ascertain the degree to which he is willing to advocate his position. Ask him:

> *"How will you proceed with the information? Will you be taking it to an individual, or to a committee?"*

If he's taking the information to a committee, coach him to go to each committee member, just as he would with a solo decision maker. This is because each committee member must be treated as if he has total decision-making power, and, accordingly, you must determine the criteria for each member.

4. Next, determine his level of commitment toward purchasing the product by asking a question like:

> *"Are you prepared to inform your boss* [or each committee member] *that you recommend purchasing this product?"*

or

> *"What is your history in terms of making recommendations to him* [them]*? Have you ever done that before?"*

or

> *"Does he* [do they] *usually listen to what you*

recommend?"

or

"What will you say if there is disagreement with your recommendation?"

5. Ask:

"What questions do you think will be asked?"

6. Ask:

"What criteria do you think will be important to him [each of them]*?"*

7. Ask:

"What objections do you think will be raised?"

8. Ask:

"How will you respond to his [their] *questions and objections?"*

For all practical purposes, what you are doing is "rehearsing" the influencer before he meets with the decision maker in order to prepare him to properly represent you. Bring to the surface all possible concerns, including the fact that your price is not the lowest whenever that is the case. The better the job you do of rehearsing him, the greater your chances are of making the sale.

In effect, you must treat the influencer as your "interim" customer while at the same time coaching him to become your "inside salesperson," which will happen if your product is a solution to *his* PAIN. You must remember that the influencer likely has his own PAIN in relation to the decision-making process. He may be worried that he will not convey the information to the decision maker correctly, or he may be concerned that he won't be able to answer all of the decision maker's questions. In both cases he would feel inadequate and fear that the decision maker will perceive him as not doing his job properly.

Your goal is to lead the influencer to discover *his* PAIN, and in the process bond with him and convey your willingness to help him accomplish his goal. This is another use of the triangle that we referred to previously in Figure 12.

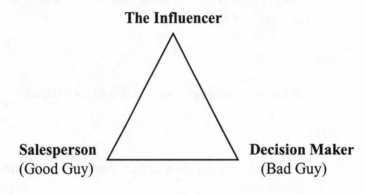

The Influencer

Salesperson   **Decision Maker**
(Good Guy)   (Bad Guy)

Figure 13

You pose as the "good" guy who is willing to help him out by meeting with the "bad" guy, that is, the decision maker who has the power to make him feel inadequate.

If this attempt fails, your last strategy can be to work to get the "last look." Ask the influencer how many other salespeople he will be requesting information from. Let's say, for instance, he responds that there will be two other parties involved. You simply ask him,

"Would it make any sense for you to get the in-

*formation that you need from the others first?
Then, if you'd like, you and I can meet to make
sure that you're comparing apples to apples,
and I can brief you for your meeting with the
boss to help you do the best job possible."*

The point is, because you position yourself as his *helper* to alleviate *his* PAIN, he is much more willing to cooperate.

The "last look" strategy also works well when the required information includes a bid or a quote. By getting the influencer to agree that you will be the *last* salesperson to whom he talks before going to the decision maker, you have increased manyfold your chances of making the sale.

Determining the Decision-Making Criteria

Regardless of whether salespeople are interfacing with the decision maker or the influencer, they often mistakenly assume that their prospect understands the product complexities sufficiently to make a truly informed buying decision. The truth of the matter is that much of the time he does not. Furthermore, when prospects don't know their own criteria for buying, they invariably try to lead the salesperson around to the subject of price. Price, like the weather, is something that is comfortable for them to talk about. It's the easiest path to take rather than reveal the PAIN that comes from their lack of knowing what specific criteria they should base their decision upon.

This lack of fully understanding the criteria upon which to make a buying decision is one of the primary reasons why customers comparison shop. They are trying to gather enough information about a product to feel comfortable—and confident—that they are making an informed decision. While this is totally understandable, the downside is that the more they shop around and the more information they collect, the less aware they are of their PAIN, and the more price conscious they become.

The key here is for salespeople to be aware that there is a real difference between (1) helping the buyer determine his criteria for making a decision, and (2) presenting product information to him. Confusing the two is an invisible black hole into which sellers are too often pulled. When a customer says, "Tell me about your product," what he really means is, "Give me some criteria to help me make my decision." The tendency for the salesperson is to take the buyer literally at this point and begin to present, which is a horrendous mistake. The Leadership Seller, on the other hand, must interpret the buyer's request for information as a clear indication of his PAIN, specifically his fear of making a poor decision because he is uninformed.

> *The ability to help a customer determine his decision-making criteria without presenting product knowledge is one of the most powerful skills in all of Leadership Selling!*

To accomplish this, make absolutely sure that *you* understand his criteria for making a buying decision through the questions that you ask. As you come to understand these factors, so does the buyer become conscious of his own criteria. As a result, his desire to shop around for information dissipates since the void of what he was *really* looking for—namely, the important criteria upon which to make a decision—has now been filled. Accordingly, his insistence that price is the primary issue diminishes in importance.

    To clarify further how to help the buyer determine his decision-making criteria, let's examine how the process plays out in terms of writing a proposal. We begin by saying that the ideal situation is to meet with the actual decision maker and therefore bypass the need to submit a proposal at all. This should always be the goal.

    There are times, however, when a written proposal is appropriate, and whenever this is the case, the question on your mind must be, "What does this person need to have in front of him in order to make a decision?" His answer is typically ambiguous, and must be accurately quantified. The following conversation is one example of the proper way to proceed:

SP: *"What do you need to see in order to make an informed decision?"* (a request for the decision-making criteria)

Buyer: *"I'll be looking for the best value for my money."* (a generalized response that, though no doubt true, is ambiguous and without substance)

SP: *"I understand—I'd be looking for the same."* (softening statement to keep the customer OK) *"What criteria will you be using to determine the best value?"* (clear up all vague terms)

Buyer: *"It must meet our service specifications at a competitive price."* (buyer is clarifying his statement and at the same time learning more about his own criteria for making a decision)

SP: *"That sounds fair."* (softening statement)
"What do we need to put in writing to meet your service specifications and to be competitively priced?" (further define specific criteria)

Buyer: *"Our service specifications are X, Y and Z, and the price must be within five percent of the competition's."* (buyer continues to become clearer in defining the criteria that are important to him)

SP: *"I appreciate your telling me that."* (stroke, keep him OK)
"What will it mean to you if my proposal meets both of these criteria?" (hypothetical question to determine the buyer's level of commitment)

Buyer: *"It will depend on what the other proposals have to offer."* (hasn't thought about other criteria until now; more vague words; if you let this statement slide by without challenging it, the customer will almost certainly revert to price when making his final decision)

SP: *"That makes sense."* (keep him OK)
"What might they have to offer in addition to service and price that would be important to you?" (clear up all ambiguity)

Buyer: *"That's difficult to answer. I guess I'm not sure."* (key point—buyer doesn't know what the rest of his criteria are, hence is looking for help)

SP: *"I can understand that."* (keep him OK)
"Some people in your situation are also concerned about _____. Would that be important to you?" (introduces a new criterion for the buyer to think about, one in fact that highlights one of your strong selling points, yet without presenting the details of the features and benefits which the buyer could easily steal)

Buyer: *"Actually, _____ could be very important."* (sudden awareness of another decision-making criterion)

SP: *"Can you tell me why that would be important to you?"* (a subtle way to ask permission to ask the next question, while at the same time asking a vertical, open-ended question in search of the buyer's PAIN)

This is the process that a Leadership Seller must use to keep his customer OK and lead him to the discovery of the criteria that are important to him. Once a salesperson has defined all such criteria, he is then in position to tailor his written proposal to the exact solutions that will solve the buyer's PAIN. Since the competition will not likely have qualified the buyer's decision-making criteria nearly so thoroughly, the Leadership Seller's odds for making a sale are obviously many times greater than they might have otherwise been.

The written proposal is, in effect, a safety net that catches anything that you might have missed in the selling interaction. You may have noticed from the comments in the previous buyer/salesperson conversation that the process of determining the buyer's criteria utilizes many other steps in the system. It is this fact—namely, that the written proposal necessitates an aggregate application of the entire system—that makes it such a powerful selling tool.

Many proposals of course are verbal rather than written, yet this fact by itself does not change the way you would proceed in determining the buyer's decision-making criteria. The only real difference in the end is that you are not required to submit it in writing. You still must ask what his criteria are, clarify his answers, keep him OK, ask for his level of commitment, and so on.

We are often asked whether this process has application in retail sales, and the answer is clearly yes, especially when the customer begins to ask questions. Whenever this happens, he is in fact trying to collect and sift out the product information that he values—that is, he is attempting to clarify in his own mind what the really important criteria are. Therefore, it is quite possible for a retail salesperson to handle a buyer's questions with this same line of questioning:

Buyer: *"I'm shopping for a lawnmower—what can you tell me about the models that you carry?"*

SP: *"I'd be happy to answer that question. First let me ask you—what factors are important to you in a lawnmower?"*

Depending on which factors he tells you are especially important to him, you can get a sense as to whether he is an experienced or inexperienced buyer with regard to lawnmowers. If, for instance, he refers to criteria A, B, C, D, and so on, then you probe for PAIN about each of these points. If, however, he says something like,

Buyer: *"I don't know very much about lawnmowers,"*

he needs your help in determining what factors he should be considering. Therefore, you must help raise his awareness of the relevant criteria he should be considering, which is *not* the same as presenting. Simply respond:

SP: *"Many people are concerned about whether it is self-propelled or not. Is that important to you?"*

In this way, you are leading him through the establishment of his own essential criteria—which, remember, always reflects his PAIN—instead of giving him important information that he can steal and/or use against you. You merely continue the process by creating new categories in your search for his PAIN until you have found enough to solidify a contract (Chapter 18), and close the sale.

Again, when you suggest to the customer new criteria that he might want to consider, this is a great opportunity for you to lead with your strong selling points. For example, if your service is better than your competitor's service, you'd want to say to the buyer:

SP: *"Some people are concerned about service. Is service important to you?"*

If he responds that it is important, then by no means should you start telling him about your wonderful service. Rather, ask him:

SP: *"Can you tell me more about that?"*

This universal question, or the use of a similar open-ended question, allows him to open up and discuss his PAIN.

In Summary

Always remember that the primary goal in the decision step is to meet with the actual decision maker. Much time is wasted and many frustrations occur as a result of presenting to non-decision makers. You must not naively accept information that it is impossible to meet with the decision maker as if it were the eleventh commandment. If you are determined enough and creative enough, there is usually a way to make it happen.

In those situations where all efforts to meet with the decision maker have failed, you have nevertheless been able to talk with the influencer, who has an impact on the final decision. Your most powerful selling approach in this event is to skillfully rehearse the influencer. You do this by leading him through a series of questions that define the decision-maker's buying criteria until you have sufficient information to write an airtight proposal.

Leadership Sellers will realize as they become proficient in the execution of the decision step that **there can be more opportunity here for the discovery of the buyer's PAIN than in any other step in the system.** Therefore, the decision step must not be taken lightly, as many salespeople are inclined to do. Rather, it must be assigned the utmost importance if one hopes to master the Leadership Selling system.

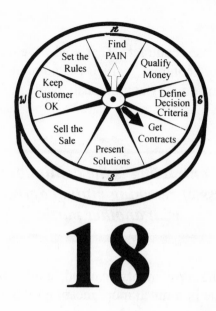

18

Ongoing Contracting

Salespeople often feel that buyers don't value the seller's time, and that buyers frequently fail to honor their commitments. The solution to both of these concerns is to acquire the skills inherent in ongoing contracting.

In order to understand the concept of ongoing contracting, it helps to keep in mind that the word contract can be used both as a noun and as a verb. Normally we think of contract in its noun form, especially as it refers to a signed document which binds two parties in some legal way.

The word "contract" in Leadership Selling, on the other hand, refers more to a *process* for communicating than to a written contract. That's why we emphasize the *verb* usage of "contract," which is a communication technique that you employ continuously while interacting with a customer.

> **Contracting is the continuous process of reaching mutual agreements with another party.**

Based on the agreements reached, communication can then continue in a much more meaningful and productive way.

Clearing Up the Ambiguity

Two stories come to mind, the second of which is true and the first obviously is not.

A man was driving along a country road when he came upon a slow-moving truck carrying a load of pigs. As he approached the truck, one of the pigs fell off the back of the truck and ran across the field. The man, thinking he would do a good deed for the day, chased down the pig, returned it to his car, and sped down the road to catch up with the pig farmer.

Moments later he was pulled over by a policeman for speeding. When he explained to the officer that he was just trying to help out the farmer, the policeman said, "Okay, that was a nice gesture on your part. Tell you what, if you'll take the pig to the zoo, I'll let you off the hook this time." Feeling very grateful, the man agreed to the officer's request.

The next day the same man was driving down the same road and was pulled over by the same officer in the same place. "What did I do now?" the man inquired, "I wasn't driving too fast!" "That's true," said the officer, "but why do you still have the pig in the front seat? I thought I told you to take him to the zoo." "I did just as you said," answered the man, "but we had so much fun I decided that today I'd take him to the ballgame."

A twelve-year-old girl's parents both worked during the day. When she returned home from school one fall afternoon, she found a note in the kitchen that read:

> *Wash five potatoes, stick a fork in each one, put them in the oven at 4:00, and turn the oven to 350°.*

When the mother arrived home at 5:30, she was furious when she found five potatoes with a red-hot fork protruding from each one *while still baking in the oven!*

Many words in the English language convey more than one meaning and therefore allow for a variety of interpretations. Some of them, in fact, are so vague that any number of misinterpretations can occur.

Buyers are accustomed to using both types—those with multiple meanings and those whose definitions are ambiguous—to disguise their PAIN from salespeople. Because of this, sellers must make a conscious effort to not let such words pass uncontested. Rather, they must immediately clarify any words or concepts that are easily misinterpreted. Doing so keeps communication mutually clear, and increases the likelihood of reaching stronger agreements. This process of asking the buyer to redefine the meaning of his words is a big part of the concept of ongoing contracting.

Words with More Than One Meaning

Many words in our language have more than one meaning. Take the word "moccasin," for example, which is both a type of shoe and a poisonous snake. "Light" means both the opposite of heavy and the opposite of dark.

When a buyer uses a word that has different meanings, you must ask for a clarification as to what he means. If he says, for example, "I must talk to my boss about this matter," what exactly does he mean by "talk?" Does he mean "inform," "recommend," "ask permission," or what?

Another instance might be when a buyer says, "We are very loyal to our vendors." What does "loyal" really mean? It might mean that (1) he never considers another supplier under *any* circumstances; (2) he discusses with his current supplier his reasons for switching before actually making the change; or (3) he truly wants to make a switch to another vendor, fears it will offend his current supplier, and doesn't know how to handle the situation.

The point is to not assume that you know what your customer intended whenever he uses any word that could possibly convey a double meaning. Instead, you must ask him to explain exactly what he meant before moving on in the discussion.

Clearing up the ambiguity is relatively straightforward—you simply ask what meaning was intended. Your actual words could be:

"Which means?"

"When you say _____, what exactly do you mean?"

"I'm not clear about what you meant by _____."

"Do you mind clarifying _____?"

"Can you tell me that in another way?"

Asking questions about "meaning" is fundamental to effective contracting. You can understand, no doubt, how this relates to your search for the customer's PAIN. By asking him what he means by certain words, phrases, concepts, etc., you are probing deeper into his feelings, and therefore moving closer to his PAIN.

Vague Words

Some words are extremely ambiguous, and customers purposely use them to avoid making commitments to salespeople. Consider the following interaction:

SP: *"Would you like to set an appointment to talk about our product line?"*

Buyer: *"Possibly."*

The buyer is intentionally choosing to be noncommital by using this vague word. He might have also said *"Maybe," "Perhaps,"* or *"Someday."* In all such cases, the salesperson must "contract" about the meaning of these words by asking clarifying questions like "Which means?" " *'Possibly'* means?" and so on. By doing so, he keeps the meaning mutually clear. The result is that solid agreements can be reached, and the conversation can move forward with mutual understanding.

It should be noted that the problem is not just how to clear up ambiguous words, but how to *recognize* them in the first place. They are so commonplace in our everyday language that we are often unaware of when they are being used. Before learning to clear up the meaning of vague words, Leadership Sellers must first learn to *hear*—that is, *detect*—such words. Otherwise, the customer can continue to use them deliberately to his advantage.

With this in mind, some of the more common vague words that must be questioned include, but by no means are limited to:

maybe	possibly	perhaps
sometime	someday	in due time
soon	we'll see	good
bad	right	wrong
better	best	important
worse	considering	it depends
not sure	hopefully	reasonable
fair	it's likely	I'll think on it

Once you learn to identify these types of words and phrases, the rule is simply to:

Never move forward in the sales interview until the buyer's ambiguous words are mutually understood!

For example:

SP: *"Would you like to set an appointment to talk about our product line?"*

Buyer: *"Possibly."*

SP: *"Which means?"*

Buyer: *"It depends on when it would be."*

SP: *"When would be best for you?"*

Buyer: *"Soon."*

SP: *"And by 'soon' you mean?"*

Buyer: *"Within the week."*

SP: *"Would Friday at two o'clock work for you?"*

Buyer: *"That would be fine; see you then."*

Is there any reader who would prefer "possibly" or "soon" to "Friday at two o'clock?"

Contracting on the Hypothetical Playing Field

In Chapter 15, rule 20, we discussed the subject of framing your questions in hypothetical language as a strategy for uncovering the buyer's PAIN. This is because it is often safer for a person to respond to a hypothetical situation than to an actual one. Questions that begin with:

"If...?"

"What if...?"

"Let's pretend that..."

and so on, allow a buyer to discuss his thoughts and feelings with the security of knowing that he can always "take back" what he said if it is to his benefit to do so.

Just as hypothetical language is valuable for leading a buyer to his PAIN, it is also effective for clarifying his level of commitment. The difference in the latter case is that the motive behind your use of hypothetical language is *commitment*-oriented rather than *PAIN*-oriented. Although you would never actually use these words, in a generic sense, hypothetical contracting establishes reciprocity in the relationship—*If **I** do X, then what are **you** willing to do?*

The Birth of Hypothetical Contracting

The whole concept of "closing" a sale tends to carry with it a negative stigma to the buyer. Traditionally, closing has meant bringing pressure to bear on the prospect, often in some "gimmicky" way. Examples include the impending-event close ("the price goes up on Monday"), the alternative-choice close ("would you like it delivered on Wednesday or Friday?"), the Ben Franklin close (the salesperson lists the pros and cons of purchasing his product, then points out that the pros outweigh the cons), and so on. Over time, customers grew wise to these and other overused closing strategies, and, as a result, such strategies began to lose their effectiveness.

Then came the innovative attempt to trial-close through the use of such hypothetical questions as:

"If I could show you a way to _____,
will you buy?"

"If my product can solve the problem that you've
discussed with me, are you ready to tell me yes or
no today?"

"If I can deliver this product to meet your dead-
line, are you ready to do business together?"

While such closing strategies are taught in seminars across the country every day and are currently used
by countless salespeople, in our view they are bittersweet
pills for customers to swallow. They are sweet because
they are hypothetical, and customers get to play momen-
tarily in the imaginary world. They are bitter, however,
because customers don't get to play for long, since the last
part of each question brings them back to the pressure of
cold, hard reality—namely, "Will you buy?" or some other
version of directly asking for the order.

In Leadership Selling, trial closes are replaced with
nonthreatening hypothetical questions where the customer
is totally free to explore his options rather than feeling
"pinned against the wall," so to speak. In other words, the
customer has the opportunity to tell the salesperson what
direction he *wants* to take with absolutely no fear of super-
imposed pressure.

The seller could say, for example, after finding the
buyer's PAIN,

"Let's suppose I could take care of the problems

*that we've discussed, **what would happen then?***"

or

"*...**what would you want to happen next?***"

or

"*...**where would we go from there?***"

or

"*...**what would you like me to do?***"

Such questions are nonthreatening because they are both hypothetical *and* open. They allow the customer to feel in control, even though categorically he can only go in one of two directions. Either he will be ready to close, in which case he will say something like, "then we'd write up an order"; or he is not ready to close, in which case he will tell you what objection or objections remain. If he does have objections, you would go back into your PAIN-finding mode of asking questions to uncover the feelings beneath his objections.

By asking the buyer open-ended hypothetical questions, *you* don't have to overcome your customer's objections, *he* does. He does this by examining his own objections and deciding what course of action he wants to take. Again, this approach gives him the feeling of being in control, even though you are really in control by the fact that you are leading him through the use of ongoing contracting to a definite decision of either yes or no.

An Example of Ongoing Contracting

The following dialogue is an illustration of how ongoing contracting actually works. While there are several Leadership Selling techniques at work here, the real point of the example is to show how a sales call unfolds when you employ hypothetical questions that are open-ended. Notice that the salesperson never tries to overcome the customer's objections. This is what traditional selling systems tend to do ad nauseam. Instead, he leads the customer to raise, *and* overcome, his own objections.

SP: *"You've said that you're worried about the condition of your existing equipment and that you're going to have to do something to correct it."* (a clear indication of the buyer's PAIN) *"When you say 'do something,' can you help me understand better what you mean?"*

Buyer: *"We'll either have to recondition it or replace it."*

SP: *"If you could do what you really wanted to do in this situation, what would that look like?"*

Buyer: *"I think I'd replace it all."*

SP: *"If there were a reason not to replace all of your existing equipment, what would it be?"*

Buyer: *"I'm afraid my partner might not go along with my point of view."*

SP: *"Please tell me about 'afraid.'"*

Buyer: *"He is extremely frugal and wants to get the most for his money. He leans toward reconditioning it."*

SP: *"What would you want to do about that?"*

Buyer: *"I'd want to talk to him about his concerns."*

SP: *"If you were to do that, what do you think he'd say?"*

Buyer: *"I think he'd be very concerned about the capital outlay."*

SP: *"It sounds like it's going to be next to impossible to sway him to your position."*

Buyer: *"That's probably true* [long pause], *unless I can convince him that it would be more cost-effective to purchase new equipment than to keep repairing the old."*

SP: *"Do you think he'd agree with you then?"*

Buyer: *"I'm quite sure that he would."*

SP: *"How do you see this unfolding?"*

Buyer: *"I think that's where you could help me. Do you have any data I could show him that would support my argument?"*

SP: *"Sure, but would that be enough for your partner? What if he asks you questions that you can't answer from the data?"*

Buyer: *"You've got a good point. I don't know what I'd do."*

SP: *"Would it make any sense for me to meet with both of you to help with questions he might ask that you can't answer?"*

Buyer: *"That makes a lot of sense. When could you do that?"*

SP: *"Like you, I'm very busy, but I'd sure like to help you out. Before we check to see if there's a time available, let me ask you this. If the three of us were to meet, what do you think would be the outcome of that meeting?"*

Buyer: *"We'd probably talk it over after you leave and decide what the best option is for us."*

SP: *"I can sure understand that. Regardless of which way you decide to go, what would come next?"*

Buyer: *"If I know my partner, he'll want to get two or three other quotes to make sure we're getting the best deal."*

SP: *"It sounds like the two of you are going to have to feel comfortable with the finances of such a big decision."*

Buyer: *"Absolutely!"*

SP: *"Do I understand correctly that you and your partner agree that something must be done,*

one way or the other?"

Buyer: *"That's right."*

SP: *"Great—when do you think we could sit down and talk?"*

Buyer: *"First thing tomorrow morning in our weekly meeting. Could you make it then?"*

SP: *"I'm sorry, I have a previous commitment for that time. What would be a good alternative for you?"*

Buyer: *"Could you make our meeting next week?"*

SP: *"Yes, I can. Let's plan on that."*

(The sales interview continues at the next meeting with all three parties present. Because there are now two buyers involved, we refer to the buyer in the preceding portion of the conversation as Buyer 1, and to his partner as Buyer 2.)

SP: *"Thank you for the opportunity to meet with the two of you.* (Addressing Buyer 1) *May we begin with reviewing why you decided to invite me to this meeting?"*

Buyer 1: *"I thought it would be a good idea for the three of us to talk rather than for you to communicate with my partner through me."*

SP: (Addressing Buyer 2) *"I heard your partner's concerns when we talked last week—that he'd like to replace all of your existing equipment, but he knows that that's going to be a sizable capital out-*

lay. Are those your concerns also?"

Buyer 2: *"I'm thinking that perhaps reconditioning our present equipment might be a better way to go."*

SP: *"I understand. What do you see as being the advantages of taking that route?"*

Buyer 2: *"It boils down strictly to money. I just don't see how we can afford to purchase new equipment."*

SP: *"I can appreciate your concern. Let me ask you this, is there any negative to reconditioning your equipment rather than replacing it?"*

Buyer 2: *"Certainly—it won't last as long, and in a few years we'll be facing this same situation again."*

Buyer 1: *"That's exactly why I lean toward buying new equipment."*

SP: *"Hypothetically, what if it were possible to finance the purchase of new equipment in such a way that you could handle the monthly payments? Would you want to talk more about that?"*

Buyer 2: *"I'm sure we would, but is that even a possibility?"*

SP: *"I'd have to know much more about your situation before I could answer that with any accuracy, but my hunch is that it may be a viable solution."*

Buyer 2: *"That's very interesting. What would you need to know in order to check that option out?"*

SP: *"I'd need to know all the criteria that you would base your final decision on, including the amount of money you could budget per month for a payment. Let me ask if what your partner said is accurate, that you'd want to get other quotes before making a decision?"*

(In most situations, you cannot prevent your prospects from securing other proposals because of the "commoditization" of the market. You must therefore exert the effort, first, to accurately determine the decision-making criteria of the buyer so that your written proposal hits the bull's-eye, and second, to try and secure the "last look." Let's get back to where we were in the dialogue.)

Buyer 2: *"Yes, I'd want to get two or three other quotes."*

SP: *"That sounds fair. I'd like to make two requests, then. First, since you're going to be getting other quotes, what would you think of scheduling another meeting **after** you have the other quotes so that when I present mine, I can help you decipher exactly what they mean and make sure that you are getting the best deal possible?"*

Buyer 2: *"That's fine with me."*

Buyer 1: *"I agree."*

SP: *"Second, so that I can be ready with my quote, let me see if I fully understand the criteria that you're going to use to make the decision. Meeting your budget is a first consideration, I understand. What range will the payment have to fall between in order to buy new equipment?"*

Buyer 2: *"Between five and six thousand per month."*

SP: *"And if I can work out a financing plan that fits this price range, what else would you be concerned about?"*

Buyer 1: *"The quality of the equipment. We wouldn't want inexpensive equipment that will break down easily and cause us other problems."*

SP: *"That sounds wise. What will you need to see in the proposal that would indicate quality equipment?"*

Buyer 1: *"It would have to be equal to or better than the equipment that we're replacing."*

SP: *"What is the make of your current equipment?"*

Buyer 2: *"Brand XYZ."*

SP: *"And how will you decide whether my equipment is equal to or better than Brand XYZ?"*

Buyer 1: *"We'd need specifications on factors 1, 2, 3, 4, 5, and so on."*

Once the criteria are fully determined so as to prepare a written proposal, all that remains is to set the last-look appointment when you can both present your proposal and consult with the buyer(s) as to the best solution to their problem.

The Advantages of Ongoing Contracting

Without question, ongoing contracting is one of the most powerful strategies in all of selling. It:

- removes virtually all perceived pressure from the selling situation.

- allows your customer to lower his guard and be open with you.

- keeps him OK by giving him the *feeling* of being in control.

- assists in probing for deeper levels of PAIN.

- keeps the communication clear at all times.

- positions you to reach well-defined agreements and establish commitments as you proceed.

- eliminates TIOs and other forms of indecisiveness.

- gives you ultimate control of the selling interaction.

Incremental Selling

One of the big mistakes that many salespeople make is to ask for larger commitments than the buyer is ready to give early on in the sales cycle. Exceptions include inexpensive items and/or products that are sold using a one-call close. For the majority of products in the marketplace, however, buyers are not willing to purchase "in a single bound," so to speak. Most buying decisions evolve over a period of time and progress through a series of steps.

It is important therefore in Leadership Selling to lead the buyer through these sequential stages of the sale. The way to accomplish this is by attaining a progressive series of small commitments from the buyer as opposed to asking for one or two major commitments. This process of leading a buyer through a series of lesser commitments is what we call "incremental" selling. In effect, it is selling to the customer in small pieces, or increments, each portion of which becomes a passageway to the next increment.

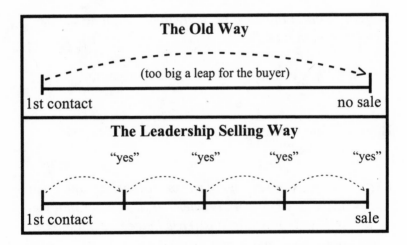

Figure 14

The concept of incremental selling blends well with the two previously discussed techniques of ongoing contracting—clearing up the ambiguity and asking open-ended hypothetical questions. For example, the question *"If we could take care of the problems you've just dis-*

cussed, what would happen next?" in effect defines the next increment. Assuming you've eliminated words with double or vague meanings, his response will indicate the direction (either to "stop" or "move forward"), which is always the goal.

　　　　To illustrate, let's look at two examples. In the first scenario, the seller leads the buyer to an eventual "no," and in the second, the seller leads the buyer to the next increment.

First Scenario: Getting to "No"

SP:　　*"Given what we've discussed so far, what comes next?"*

Buyer:　*"I don't think we're ready to do anything at this point in time."*

SP:　　*"When you say, 'I don't think we're ready,' you mean?"*

Buyer:　*"That it's not going to happen for at least six months."*

SP:　　*"If this were six months from now, what would you want me to do? And remember, I'd rather that you tell me 'no' if your answer is indeed no than to be polite and lead me on."*

Buyer:　*"Okay, then, no."*

SP:　　*"Thank you for being direct with me; not very many people can do that. If I can ever be of help, please feel free to give me a call."*

Remember, "no" is a perfectly acceptable answer in Leadership Selling. To be polite and not hurt the salesperson's feelings, "suspects" are accustomed to softening their intended "no" with white lies and vague generalizations, such as "I like what you've shown me—let me think it over and I'll get back to you." Responses of this type sound enough like a "yes" to many, many salespeople that they continue to pursue the people who say them. By and large, chasing such individuals is a total waste of the salesperson's time. And given the warp-speed economy in which we do business, nothing is more important in a salesperson's work life than his time for working with serious prospects.

So again, "yes" is the best answer you can hear from a potential customer; "no" is the second-best answer; and "I want to think it over" (TIO) is totally unacceptable, and must be converted into either a "yes" or a "no."

Second Scenario: Setting Up the Next Increment

SP: *"Given what we've discussed so far, what comes next?"*

Buyer: *"It depends."*

SP: *"On?"*

Buyer: *"On whether the people who actually operate this machine accept it."*

SP: *"And if they do?"*

Buyer: *"Then I'd be ready to do business with you."*

SP: *"I sure appreciate that. How exactly were you*

227

hoping to find out if your people will accept it?"

Buyer: *"I'd want them to try it."* (thus defining the
next increment)

SP: *"That sounds reasonable. Could I ask what it
would look like to have them try it?"*

Buyer: *"I'd like everyone involved to use it for a day or
two to see if it meets with their approval."*

SP: *"How soon would you like to do that?"*

Buyer: *"At your earliest convenience."*

SP: *"Suppose we install it next Monday, and on Friday
we meet to see what everyone thinks. If they all
like it, what would happen then?"*

Buyer: *"We would sign the papers!"*

SP: *"And if anyone has concerns?"*

Buyer: *"We'd have to address their concerns to see if they
can be taken care of."*

SP: *"Fair enough."*

~

One of the most valuable aspects of incremental
selling is that, again, the buyer does not perceive pressure
from the salesperson. Within reason, of course, he is at
total liberty to define his next increment, whatever that

happens to be for him. Since he does not feel high-pressured, he is free to explain exactly what steps you must take to sell him the product in question as a solution to his PAIN.

You are well on your way to making a sale as long as the increment that the buyer suggests is moving toward that end. If, however, he shows no desire to move forward, then you must ask him if it's over. He will either (a) answer "no," (b) give you another objection that he needs to work through before proceeding to the next step, (c) answer in vague terms that will have to be clarified, or (d) tell you "yes, it's over."

The bottom line is never to accept maybe's, TIOs, and other wishy-washy words that convey indecisiveness on the buyer's part. In one form or another, you must only accept:

- *"Yes, I'll buy from you," or*

- *"No, it's over," or*

- *"Let's move forward by taking the next step."*

By leading the buyer to one of these three options, ongoing contracting ensures that there will not be any unexpected surprises later on.

A word of caution at this point: There are certain situations where a TIO *can be* the next legitimate step for the buyer. The way to determine if this is the case is to make sure the meeting ends with a clear contract as to who is going to do what, when they will do it, what the results will be of everyone doing what they committed to do, and so on. If a salesperson receives quantifiable answers to these kinds of specific questions, then the TIO is real and must be treated as a valid increment for the buyer. On the other hand, if he isn't willing to give clear answers to your questions, he is probably trying to tell you "no," in which case your best move is to call the game (rule 22) and ask him if that is his intention.

Predetermined Increments

Sometimes interested buyers don't know what should come next when you ask them what they want to do. Such individuals will expect you to give them a recommendation, and will look to you for help on how to move forward in their buying process.

This is an area where you must exercise extreme caution so that your suggestion doesn't turn your product into a mere "try before you buy" marketing scheme. It would be inappropriate for a Leadership Salesperson, for example, to respond as follows:

SP: *"Given what we've just discussed, what would you like to see happen next?"*

Buyer: *"I'm not sure—what do you recommend?"*

SP: *"I think you should install it for a week and try it to see if you like it."*

This is precisely what *not* to do. The first infraction that the salesperson committed was to phrase his recommendation as a "should." One must never "should-upon" his customers. Not only is it condescending to do so, it also exerts too much pressure on them. Second, and more importantly, he must never offer the enticement of "try before you buy" without first having a clear contract as to what comes next after the trial period expires.

When one abides by the rules of Leadership Selling, here is how the same interaction would transpire:

SP: *"Given what we've just discussed, what would you like to see happen next?"*

Buyer: *"I'm not sure—what do you recommend?"*

SP: *"Would it make any sense to install the equipment for a week in order for you to find out if it's really going to do the job for you?"*

Buyer: *"That makes sense to me."*

SP: (getting a solid contract first) *"Good. Do you think you'd know by then if investing in the equipment is the right choice for you?"*

Buyer: *"I don't see why I wouldn't."*

SP: *"And if it is the right choice for you, what would you want to happen then?"*

Buyer: *"I'd like to meet on Friday to finalize the deal."*

SP: *"Great. What time would you like to meet on Friday?"*

This is what Leadership Selling is all about. The customer was **led** to believe that it was *his* idea to take the next step, that *he* made the decision, and that *his* decision

231

was a wise one. Furthermore, the salesperson led the customer to making a clear commitment that after one week a "yes" or "no" decision will be given.

The idea is for you to have two or three predetermined increments so that you can move your prospect forward in the event that he needs guidance on what to do next. To accomplish this, you must look at your specific industry and determine what those key increments are for you. In one business, for example, the first increment may be a tour of the plant. In another, it might be a chance to talk with other satisfied customers. And in still another, perhaps it would be an opportunity to do a small amount of business in order to build enough trust to move forward and take the next, larger step.

A good rule of thumb for you to follow is to first let the customer define the next increment that makes sense to him. When he struggles with deciding what to do, only then do you offer a recommendation, and ask him if he agrees with your suggestion as to how to proceed.

These three components of ongoing contracting, namely,

- clearing up the ambiguity,

- asking for commitments in hypothetical language, and

- selling your product in increments,

converge to form a dynamic selling triad. When you add these components to the other strategies in Leadership Selling, the balance of power that we referred to in Chapter 8 will be forever tipped in your favor.

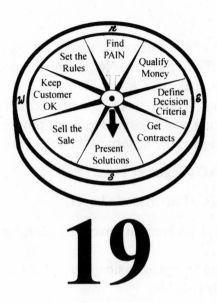

19

Presenting Is Pro-ACT-ing

Traditionally, every sales call contains three essential components:

- presenting product knowledge ("Telling"),

- qualifying the buyer ("Asking"), and

- closing the sale ("Closing").

While Telling (T)—that is, talking about features, advantages, and benefits—has been, and will continue to be, an integral part of the sales call, the single most important factor about **Telling** is the order in which it occurs in relation to Asking (**A**) and Closing (**C**).

In our view, three specific combinations of Telling, Asking, and Closing represent progressive stages in the evolution of the history of the sales call.

- **TAC** (Beginner Level)

- **ATC** (Intermediate Level)

- **ACT** (Advanced Level—Leadership Selling)

To understand this progression better, let's examine each stage more thoroughly.

Beginner Level: TAC

Many neophyte salespeople begin their careers doing **TAC**. When they find a "warm body" who will listen, they launch into their so-called "dog and pony" shows, Telling about all of the wonderful features and benefits that their product has to offer. At some point during their exhaustive delivery, they may or may not attempt to Ask the buyer whether he has any need for such a product. Then when the buyer begins to resist, the salesperson immediately pulls out his bag of Closing tricks in an attempt to secure the sale.

TAC-salespeople spend as much as 80 percent of their time in the Telling phase, little if any time in the Asking phase, and the remainder of their time trying to Close. So much Telling by a salesperson creates major pitfalls, and is in absolute direct violation of the basic principles of Leadership Selling. The goal, remember, is to keep the customer talking (rule 1) as you skillfully Ask questions to discover his PAIN. Doing so requires listening 75 percent of the time and talking only 25 percent of the time. Obviously, it is impossible to do this in **TAC** where the salesperson is almost totally monopolizing the conversation.

T_{ell}	A_{sk}	C_{lose}
80%	5%	15%

Intermediate Level: ATC

Few salespeople can make a living for very long using the **TAC** approach. They eventually burn out giving million-dollar presentations with little or no reward, since buyers need only say, "Let me think it over" to dismiss them. Consequently, **TAC**-salespeople tend to either drop out of sales, or they graduate to the next level—**ATC.**

ATC is a giant stride forward in the sales profession. It recognizes the importance of qualifying the buyer by **A**sking him certain questions to determine whether he is a viable candidate for making a purchase. The truth is that **ATC** is the method of choice for the majority of salespeople today. However, there are two distinct problems with adopting this outdated approach.

First, most salespeople who use **ATC** are qualifying for the buyer's "needs," typically by **A**sking a series of predetermined questions. As we discussed previously, "needs" are only a small part of what constitutes PAIN. One could "need" an operation because his appendix is infected; but his PAIN lies in his fears about what happens if he *doesn't* get the operation. The point is, we believe that most of what passes for **A**sking in **ATC** is sophomoric and superficial compared to the much more comprehensive concept of **A**sking as defined in Leadership Selling.

235

Second, once **ATC**-salespeople have qualified the buyer with their questions, their next step is to **T**ell about their product knowledge, which in our view is premature because it ignores the importance of contracting first. The buyer now has the option of using product information against the seller to evade making a commitment. This leaves the salesperson in the same position of using **C**losing tactics that are often perceived as "high-pressured" by the buyer. Though more time is given in **ATC** to the **A**sking process, still the majority of time in the sales call is spent in the **T**elling phase.

Ask	**T**ell	**C**lose
35%	50%	15%

Advanced Level—the Leadership Selling Way: ACT

Leadership Selling is fully grounded in the **ACT** approach. One could say that a true sales *pro*fessional using **ACT** is *pro*-**ACT**-ing in the fullest sense of the word!

The idea is to **A**sk questions of the buyer in order to discover his PAINful feelings as opposed to simply gathering facts, as happens in **ATC**. Having accomplished this, **A**sk open-ended hypothetical questions so that you can contract toward a **C**lose by means of getting incremental commitments along the way. Again,

> **Never *Tell* unless you first have a clear contract about what will happen when you do.**

Only after he has admitted his PAIN and he gives you a commitment to buy if you can solve it do you **T**ell how your product will remedy his problem. **T**elling, then, is simply icing on the cake to finalize the sale.

$\mathbf{A}$sk	$\mathbf{C}$lose	$\mathbf{T}$ell
80%	**5%**	**15%**

~

The key to the **ACT** approach is to make sure that the product knowledge that you present addresses the specific PAINs that the buyer has revealed. Said differently, if your product has, let's say, fifteen features and benefits, but you have discovered that the buyer has only three specific PAINs, then you would present *only* the information that pertains to those three PAINs, and nothing more.

When you give more product knowledge to the customer than that which relates directly to solving his PAIN, you invite the perception that you are more interested in talking than in being sensitive to his dilemma. Nothing frustrates a buyer more than being forced to listen to product knowledge that is not relevant to his situation. Not only might this offend him and dampen his interest in purchasing your product, but, as we mentioned earlier, you might inadvertently give him product knowledge that empowers him to find new reasons why he should not buy your product. Consider the following example:

Buyer: *"Show me what you have."*

SP: *"I have a group health insurance plan that is*

237

> *better than anything else out there. It is zero*
> *percent deductible, pays on claims within five*
> *days, and involves an absolute minimum of paper*
> *work. We can offer such a deal because we are one*
> *of three large insurance companies that merged*
> *into one, which cuts our overhead considerably."*

Buyer: *"It sounds like an excellent opportunity, but I*
prefer not to do business with companies that
have merged."

SP: *"I don't understand why you would have a problem*
with mergers. More and more companies are
merging these days. As a result, they can bring you
more benefits at competitive prices. So why not
give this some serious thought?"

Buyer: *"You have a point—let me talk it over with my*
associates, and I'll get back to you" (never to be
heard from again).

Here is a case where the salesperson is telling the
buyer information that was later used against him, namely,
that their company is a merger with two others. There is
some specific PAIN in the buyer about mergers that the
salesperson did not uncover, and that PAIN is blocking the
buyer from considering the product seriously. We can't
know for certain what that PAIN is unless we ask vertical
questions as to the *source* of the PAIN. Perhaps he experienced a previous merger that was problematic for him, or
maybe his boss has issued a mandate not to do business
with any companies that have merged. Regardless, the
point is that presenting too much information before finding the PAIN allowed the buyer to use some of that information in a way that blocked having to reveal the true

PAIN. Just remember,

> **Only *Tell* your buyer about product knowledge that is specific to *his* PAIN.**

A word of caution about how much to Tell when you are officially in that phase of the sales call. By this point you have narrowed down the product knowledge that you will present to the information that is specific to the buyer's PAIN. Even so, it is best not to reveal it all at once because if you do, you will have relinquished the opportunity to use some of that information in order to secure the sale.

It is far better to pause one-half to two-thirds of the way through the Telling phase to "take the buyer's temperature" concerning his readiness to make a final commitment. While you still have information yet to give, ask the question, "Are we getting closer or further away from what you wanted?" If he says "closer," then ask, "What else must be done to take care of your concerns?" Whatever he says, if at all possible, do it.

If, on the other hand, the buyer says, "We're getting further away," then you can be certain that you haven't yet found his PAIN. And remember—no PAIN, no sale. Therefore, you must go back in the formula to Ask and repeat the process until you get a "no" or a clear indication to move forward.

20

Selling the Sale

All salespeople can identify with the dreadful sinking feeling of having closed a sale, or so they thought, only to have the buyer unexpectedly change his mind and cancel the transaction. Often referred to as "buyer's remorse," this change of heart has caused many emotional roller coaster rides for the unsuspecting salesperson.

Using the strategy of "selling the sale" helps you prevent this situation from occurring. Assuming that you have properly performed the first seven steps of the eight-part system, namely:

1. kept your customer OK,

2. set the rules by establishing an upfront contract,

3. found the buyer's PAIN,

4. qualified for money,

5. determined the decision-making criteria,

6. contracted throughout the interview, and

7. presented specific solutions to the buyer's PAIN,

you are now in the perfect position to "sell the sale" to prevent any last-minute cancellations.

What Exactly Is "Selling the Sale?"

"Selling the sale" is in effect asking the buyer a question about the likelihood that he might change his mind and back out after he made the decision to buy. The question must be open-ended and hypothetical in order to allow the buyer to project his thoughts into the future, as follows:

SP: *"Now that you have made the decision to purchase this product, what—if anything—could happen to cause you to change your mind?"*

If the buyer has any hidden objections that have the potential of spoiling the deal, he is now likely to bring them to light. If so, you promptly go back to **Ask** to get him to examine and work through his lingering concerns. If on the other hand he can't think of anything that might change his mind, then you have in effect "sold the sale."

For all practical purposes, "selling the sale" is giving the buyer the opportunity to change his mind in your
presence rather than afterward when you no longer have
any control over the situation. When you give him the
opportunity to do so, he is far less likely to experience remorse; or if he does, he has already told you how he will
handle it.

A Prerequisite to "Selling the Sale"

Many salespeople are taken aback by the suggestion that they should proactively offer buyers the opportunity to reverse their decision to buy. They fear that the
mere mention to the buyer that he can still change his mind
may cause him to do so. Furthermore, most salespeople
have been taught repeatedly to *never* bring up negative influences that could possibly jeopardize the sale.

In Leadership Selling, however, it is essential that
you proactively confront the possibility of buyer's remorse rather than ignore it as if it did not exist. When you
learn to face head-on the risk of losing a sale by initiating
that scenario yourself, you become mentally and emotionally tough—a prerequisite to mastering Leadership Selling.

"Going for No" Revisited

In reality, "selling the sale" is another version of
"going for no," a concept that was discussed in PAIN rule
19. It is such an important principle that it merits further
mention here.

We sometimes do a word-association exercise with
salespeople where they are asked to say the first word that
comes to mind after we give them a word. If we say "hot,"

people invariably say the opposite—"cold." Likewise with up/down, in/out, light/dark, and so on—most people respond with opposites.

This same principle is reflected in many childhood disagreements, where one youngster asserts "Yes I can!" versus the other's claim of "No you can't!" and similarly with "will"/"will not," "did"/"did not," and the like. The point is that people tend naturally to think in opposites.

Leadership Selling strategically makes use of this human propensity. When you tell a customer that he won't, he spontaneously thinks that he will. When you tell him that he probably *wouldn't* be interested in X, he automatically responds that he *would* be interested. This is why we said in rule 19 that it is ironic that the more you try to get a customer to say "no," the less likely he is to actually say it.

This principle relates directly to the concept of selling the sale. The more you attempt to get customers to tell you why they might change their mind, the less likely they are to do so. All of this is to say that salespeople need not fear that customers will change their mind when they sell the sale. To the contrary, the sale will only be firmed up, which is the precise purpose of "selling the sale."

There are certain situations where "selling the sale" is unnecessary, such as with a longstanding customer whom you trust. There are three scenarios, however, where "selling the sale" is especially important:

- When you're working with a previous customer who has a history of changing his mind.

- When your "gut instinct" tells you that you don't really trust the buyer although he said "yes."

- When you have an ongoing customer with whom you do repeat business, and there is a possibility that after a period of time you may be taking him for granted.

Because this last case can sneak up on you without your being aware of it, we recommend that you make it a habit to periodically ask your repeat customers a "selling the sale" question. For instance,

SP: *"I probably don't take the time to tell you nearly enough how much I appreciate your business. Is there anything I can improve on to make sure you remain happy working with me?"*

If the customer responds with a concern, then of course, go to work immediately to address that issue. If, however, he indicates that everything is fine, then ask:

SP: *"Could I ask you to do me a big favor? If you're ever unhappy with me for any reason, would you please bring that up to me directly so that we can get it taken care of?"*

Using this approach, you are essentially selling your future sales by intentionally heading off any potential problems before they come up.

Getting the Problem on the Table

There are times when "selling the sale" necessitates that you put specific problems on the table. It may be the case, for example, that there is a competitor in the market who is intentionally undercutting your prices. As a result, you may be experiencing a rash of "back-outs" from buyers who told you "yes" but changed their minds when the lower-priced competitor passed through the area.

If this were the case, you would need to modify how you "sell the sale" by getting that particular problem on the table:

SP: *"I appreciate your decision to buy my product. If it's all right, I'd like to share with you that there is a competitor in the area who is trying to undercut our prices. If he were to call on you before this deal is finalized, how do you think you'd respond to him?"*

If he says not to worry about it and that his decision is made, you have in all likelihood just prevented a potential back-out from occurring because you put the problem on the table and projected it into the future. On the other hand, if he responds in a way that causes you to believe that he would look seriously at purchasing the competitor's product, then again, go back to **Ask** and inquire about his concerns.

To demonstrate how the techniques in Leadership Selling would proceed, let's continue with the above scenario:

Buyer: *"I'd listen closely to what he had to say. Wouldn't you if you were in my shoes?"*

SP: *"I understand how tempting that would be. Can you think of any problems that might arise if you were to buy at a lower price from a competitor who is suddenly slashing his prices?"*

Buyer: *"I guess I wouldn't know if he'd be around to service my needs tomorrow."*

SP: *"It sounds like you're telling me that the stability of our company is important to you."*

Buyer: *"Yes, I think that's true."*

SP: *"So how are you thinking you'll respond to the lower-priced competitor in the event that he calls on you?"*

Buyer: *"I'll tell him that I've already made a decision to buy from you."*

SP: *"I really appreciate that vote of confidence in me. I assure you that I'll be there in the future to help with your needs."*

~

Another problem to get on the table is when you open a new account that replaces an existing supplier. You'd want to ask:

SP: *"Thank you for your decision to buy my product. If I could, I'd like to ask what's going to happen when your existing supplier finds out that he's losing the business?"*

The point is that you must get this potential problem on the table because it is sometimes very difficult for buyers to inform their current supplier that they are changing vendors. It is important that you lead the customer to think through how he will address this uncomfortable situation. If you don't, he can easily revert to keeping his old supplier because of his discomfort with confronting the other person.

Again, the point of "selling the sale" is to bring to the surface and resolve any problem related to the possibility of the buyer changing his mind, even though by all appearances he has made a final decision. Consistent with the whole philosophy of Leadership Selling, the secret is in the setup where foresight rather than hindsight is the overarching rule.

Part V

The Required Equipment

The technology required to sell effectively today is light-years beyond where it was only a few years ago. Yet many salespeople are still naively relying on equipment that is simply outdated. PART V: THE RE-QUIRED EQUIPMENT is a brief explanation, not only of the accessories needed to fully implement the principles of Leadership Selling, but also of the appropriate attitude that is required toward technological change, as well.

21

You *Can* Teach an Old Dog New Tricks

Vince, a fifty-eight-year-old salesperson who sells time-shares, came to us recently feeling very frustrated and overwhelmed. Unfortunately, his story is not that uncommon.

"A few years ago when personal computers first became popular I thought to myself, 'Sure, they offer certain salespeople some nice options, but it doesn't seem all that important for me to learn how to use one.' More recently it seems like almost everyone in business has a com-

*puter, or at least knows how to use one, and I've been feel-
ing more and more like I'm falling behind others in my
field. Still, I let the whole matter slide until recently my
six-year-old grandson asked me to play a game on his
computer with him, and, quite frankly, I was embarrassed!
He knew more already at six than I feel like I could ever
hope to learn! I know it's time to do something about this
situation, but I'm afraid it's too late; and besides, I don't
have the slightest idea where to begin."*

Whoever said that you can't teach an old dog new
tricks was wrong. Dead wrong. The truth is that learning
is not limited by a person's age as much as by his readiness, and willingness, to learn.

The problem with learning "new tricks" is that we
humans are creatures of habit. We tend to continue doing
those behaviors that we learned to do when we first entered
the field, especially if those behaviors worked then to accomplish our desired goals. If in fact old habits die hard,
it is due in large part to our tendency to believe that since
certain behaviors worked well once, maybe if we try hard
enough now, they will work well again.

Yet in our rapidly changing world of exploding
technology, it is becoming increasingly self-evident that
old technology-related behaviors simply *do not* work as
they once did, just as old selling behaviors no longer work
as effectively as they did in the past. Who, for example,
using a typewriter could begin to keep pace today with a
competitor who uses a word processor and a printer? Anyone who is candid with himself knows that, quite literally,
such a match would be no contest.

Acquiring the Proper Perspective on Sales-Related Technology

You will recall from Chapter 4 that we discussed the concept of warp-speed change and the astronomical effect that it has on modern-day business. We did not, however, address specific ramifications that such rapid change has on the salesperson's use of technology today.

To help set the stage for that discussion, consider, for instance, that:

- In 1950, 73 percent of all U.S. employees worked in production and manufacturing, compared with only 15 percent today.

- The U.S. Department of Labor estimates that by the year 2000, at least 44 percent of all workers will be in data services gathering, processing, retrieving, and analyzing information.

- In 1991, for the first time ever, companies spent more money on computing and communications equipment than on industrial mining, farm equipment, and construction equipment combined.

- It is estimated that two-thirds of U.S. employees today work in the service sector where information is the most important product.

- What is commonly thought of as the first modern computer, and given the name ENIAC, was built in 1944. It took up more space than an 18-wheel tractor-trailer, weighed more than 17 Chevrolet Camaros, and consumed 140,000 watts of electricity. It could execute up to 500 basic arithmetic operations per second. By contrast, the 486 personal computer today runs on a tiny silicon "chip"—and this chip is about the size of a dime, weighs less than a packet of artificial sweetener, uses less than two watts of electricity, and can execute up to 54 million instructions per second!

- Today's average consumer carries more computing power in his wristwatch than existed in the entire world before 1961.

Those salespeople who have grown up within the framework of such staggering change perhaps accept it as "normal," and have learned to adapt quickly and "roll with the punches," so to speak. For those individuals who weren't brought up in the computer age, however, and who feel that they are becoming more and more technologically illiterate with each passing day, it is understandable that they feel inadequate and fearful. Yet the picture is not as bleak as it may appear.

While it is true that technological advancements can be scary, much of that fear is more related to the "fear of the unknown" than any real reason to fear the actual technology. In practice, much of that technology is something that you will likely never need or use. It's like buying a new television set with the capability of receiving hundreds of channels through satellite transmission. As impressive as this sounds, in actual practice the majority of people will use only a small fraction of its total potential.

Now this is not to say that the total capability of any given piece of technology is not valuable. There are many people who have the know-how to utilize such equipment to its fullest potential. It is to say, however, that these people represent only a small percentage of the population, and that the majority needs to know only a fraction of the equipment's capability in order to benefit from its use.

In other words, you don't need to understand the whole technological picture to take advantage of the equipment's ability to help you sell more effectively and efficiently. Learning to use sales-related technology is similar to the way that E. L. Doctorow describes the experience of writing a book. He compares it to driving at night in the fog: while you can only see as far as the headlights, you can still make it to your destination that way.

So it is with technology. You must be careful that you don't find yourself waiting for the fog to lift before you start using the technology. The fact is that for most of us, the fog will never lift. To the contrary, it promises only to get thicker. But that needn't be a deterrent. You need only take it in small bites and use what you can. You can expect the so-called "learning curve," which means that for a short time the technology will actually slow you down until you achieve a certain level of proficiency. With a little practice, however, you will soon surpass your previous level of accomplishment, the fear fades, and results ensue.

The Point

Regardless of one's age or level of technological capability, it is never too late to stretch oneself by learning new "tricks." As we said, to do so is more a matter of desire and attitude toward technology than any other factor.

The fact is that the day is coming soon when one will not be able to function in sales at all without a working knowledge of current technology. So if there is technology available in your particular area of sales that others are utilizing more and more every day but you are afraid of learning to use it, you must face that fear head-on and begin learning what you need to know in order to keep pace.

Many wonderful programs are available to help you do so. It's not a matter of "*can* you learn?" but much more, "are you *ready* to learn?" Only you can answer that question.

22

Here Today

Some readers will be well apprised of the technology that is available to salespeople today, while others will not be as well informed. Whichever is your case, we emphasize that our intention is not to suggest here that you should immediately go out and buy a specific piece of equipment in your particular area of sales. We can't properly advise you because, first, the equipment that is appropriate for you will depend upon the exact situation that you are currently in. Second, any technology that we might suggest could well become obsolete in the lapse of time, however long that may be, between the writing of this book and your reading of it. Our purpose in this chapter, therefore, is nothing more than to acquaint you with some of the current trends in technology, and the tremendous potential that exists for salespeople who learn to apply it to their jobs.

The Age of Instant Communication

Given the warp-speed economy in which we live, the speed at which communication occurs between salesperson and customer is absolutely paramount. The question is not, "Is the speed of communication important?" but rather, "Is there any way to improve communication with my customers *beyond* that of my competition?" The answer, of course, depends on the technology that your competitors are now using, and what resources are available to you to surpass them.

Much has happened in the field of communications from the standpoint of technological advancement. Consider the sheer magnitude of the following examples. The number of cellular telephone subscribers has jumped from none in 1983 to sixteen million by the end of 1993! Close to nineteen million people now carry pagers, and almost twelve *billion* messages were left in voice mailboxes in 1993 alone. Since 1987, homes and offices have added 10 million fax machines, while e-mail addresses have increased by over twenty-six million.

Pagers

There are two reasons why pagers can be a valuable communication tool for salespeople today. First, they obviously enhance your ability to respond quickly to your customer's attempts to communicate with you. Second, a

258

pager gives your customers the feeling of having a direct link with you, which adds to their feeling of importance that you give them. This is especially relevant today given the frustration that customers often experience when they try to work their way through automated telephone systems and corporate bureaucracies in their attempts to contact you.

Modems and Faxes

Fax machine to fax machine transmissions are, of course, mainstays of the work environment today. Many individuals are not aware, however, that built-in modems allow for fax-machine-to-computer, computer-to-fax-machine, and computer-to-computer facsimile transmissions, as well. By installing the appropriate software, faxes can be programmed to be sent to whole groups of people rather than to send a fax to one individual at a time.

What this means in practice is that if you want to send a monthly newsletter to each of your clients and top prospects, it is now possible to enter the newsletter into your computer fax program, designate the intended recipients, program-in the transmission time, and then leave the rest up to the machines! The advantages are that your computer can fax the newsletter in your absence, whether you are out on appointments, off work, or asleep at night.

In effect, modems and faxes allow you to leverage your time by having certain materials faxed when you are not necessarily present. The volume of information that can be transmitted in this way is staggering to the mind. One company we work with, for instance, presently faxes out over 5,500 newsletters every day!

On-Line Communications

Salespeople who can access on-line computer services are able to learn the latest information concerning their product's development and availability. They can access graphic depictions that demonstrate how certain products work, in both a still-picture and motion-picture format.

One of the clear benefits of having on-line capability is the potential for improving your presentations. For example, a risk management firm that we work with has stated that the days are over for delivering presentations in stacks of bound documents. Instead, they give all presentations and proposals to a company on diskette rather than as hard copy, and then the company processes as many copies as they desire.

Other clients are scoffing at the idea of using slide shows in presentations any longer, as it represents obsolete technology. Instead, more and more work is being done through high-level graphics and computer-based technology that is projected onto wide screens for video enhancement of the presentation.

E-Mail and Voice Mail

It used to be that a customer could go days and weeks without actually ever speaking to a salesperson who spent most of his time outside of the office, perhaps traveling or being in front of other customers. At the time, the primary means of communication was the exchange of messages through secretaries and their handwritten notes.

Today, e-mail and voice mail allow messages to be recorded and exchanged voice-to-voice without ever talking with each other directly. As a result, salespeople are able to spend more time face-to-face with customers during the day, and then work after hours to leave either e-mail or voice mail messages for them. This potential for...(time out—there may not be reason to finish this sentence because of information on product upgrade just received via fax, which follows).

F-L-A-S-H N-O-T-I-C-E: "Electronic Secretary May Make Today's Voice Mail Obsolete"

Phone services are now being developed that replace voice mailboxes with electronic assistants that can imitate the secretary's voice, as well as perform certain secretarial functions. Such systems are capable of responding to verbal commands, recognizing the caller's voice, connecting urgent callers to the appropriate person, remembering appointments, and narrating messages when asked.

Mobile Offices

More and more salespeople are equipping themselves with in-the-car fax machines and modems in order to do business during what is now commonly referred to as "windshield time." Some salespeople are even turning to mobile office vans, which are customized vans that are fully equipped with computer, fax machine, cellular phone, desk, and batteries to run the system. Those individuals who use them are able to transact business right inside the van, just as if the parties involved were sitting in the comfort of their own offices.

Technology and Processes

Technology can be used to enhance virtually every

process in Leadership Selling. Examples that demonstrate the truth of this principle follow:

- Although we did not address the subject of prospecting directly, technology certainly plays a large part in the prospecting process through the importation and use of valuable data bases, the development of tickler files, and the like.

- Technology allows for automatic phone dialing, queuing up various lists for cold calling, and again, keeping track of the data bases.

- Specific efforts can be made to keep customers feeling OK by faxing them stroke-like statements (e.g., "I certainly appreciate doing business with you."), struggling for help (e.g., "I'm not clear about what you meant when you said that you need this proposal 'soon'—can you help me out?"), and so on. Also, if you know that a certain customer likes to follow one specific athletic team, for example, you can fax him a copy of that team's schedule just to stay in touch.

- Upfront agendas can be faxed to the prospect in advance of the sales call so that he can be informed of the agenda and of what he can anticipate will occur in the meeting. The more knowledge a prospect has of what will happen when you meet with him, the less fear he has and the lower the likelihood that there will be barriers to communication when you actually arrive for the interview.

- Software technology can be used to easily store and readily retrieve the proper questionnaires and interview strategies that you intend to employ with a customer.

- Computer technology can be used extensively in the efficient preparation and customization of proposals, just as it is helpful for clarifying any misunderstandings, improving all communications, and reaching clear agreements.

- Excellent software programs are available to help salespeople and their managers identify their own behavior styles and personality traits. The more a salesperson understands his own natural style of communication, and the better he becomes at recognizing the communication patterns of others, the more effective he is in responding to each customer and developing strategies that relate specifically to him.

- One of the most important uses of technology for salespeople is the tracking of their transactions with customers and following through on those transactions. Whether it is following up after a sale has been made, developing referrals, establishing ongoing correspondence, or loading information about a customer back into the system to recall important information in the future, the value of such functions for a salesperson is immeasurable.

- We said in Chapter 12 that every salesperson must begin to view his sales job as if it were his own business. Modern computer technology gives every salesperson this opportunity because of the amount of information that he can store and access as needed.

- Technology is now available to integrate processes interdepartmentally. Whether it is the sales process integrated with inventory, or with the sales design division, or with the accounting department, all such processes can now be integrated. The point is that the salesperson is no longer all alone, "out there by himself," so to speak. Rather, through the proper use of technology, he is now able to bring along the resources of all the other departments of the company with him. Such continuity allows a company to create a "seamless" organization in the eyes of the customer. This capability gives the obvious impression that the salesperson sees the larger picture and is more fully informed, and is therefore perceived as being more helpful.

The point of discussing the application of technology to various processes is to understand that sales is not an isolated function within the larger organization as it once was. Sales has evolved into a business within a business, and must be conducted accordingly. Again, this relates to why we say that salespeople must now think as business owners do if they hope to excel in their field.

23

Gone Tomorrow

As mentioned, some of the technology that we discussed in the previous chapter might well be obsolete by the time you read this book. Such is the nature of the world today.

Change is happening so fast that it is not possible anymore for a salesperson to purchase a certain piece of equipment and be content in knowing that it will serve him well over a long period of time. It is mandatory, therefore, that salespeople develop the right perspective toward technological change that *will* serve them well, now that rapid change is here to stay. Such a perspective must include having the correct attitude about the question—whose responsibility is it to stay abreast of rapidly changing technology?

Our answer to that question is an unequivocal, "YOU are responsible, ultimately!" And because *you* are, there are two specific areas that need your immediate attention if you are not already tending to them.

Your Equipment

Part and parcel to Leadership Selling is the premise that to master the system, salespeople must become leaders themselves. As leaders, they must learn to anticipate technological requirements for working efficiently with their customers rather than wait for their employer to say, "This is what you need to do."

Initially, many salespeople resist the suggestion that they must proactively anticipate the necessary technology rather than react to their employer's directives about it. Such resistance is understandable, since traditionally employers have been responsible for giving direction to their employees. ***But this is a different world where warp-speed reigns.*** The simple truth is that many employers are in the same boat that salespeople are in today: change happens so fast that they can't begin to comprehend it all on their own, let alone furnish all of the required guidance. To the surprise of many, employers often welcome the salesperson's initiative in this regard.

In effect, this rapid rate of technological change places more and more responsibility on each individual salesperson to think as a business owner—that is, to see his sales job as being that of an independent contractor. By so doing, a salesperson positions himself to *lead* the effort to upgrade the tools of his trade rather than follow the lead of others who may well know less about it than he does.

~

    To say that you are ultimately responsible is not to say that your employer has *no* responsibility about staying technologically current. The truth is, however, that there will be two distinct types of supervisors who represent the company and to whom you might take your technological requests and concerns. One type will be progressive, forward thinking, proactive, will understand the importance of your requests, and will welcome your input. The second type will be threatened, reactive, will consider your requests to be excessive, and will discourage your initiative and veto your suggestions.

    We hope that every reader is blessed with the first type of manager. In those cases where you do take the lead and the company doesn't support you, however, you will be faced with some difficult decisions. Your choices include:

1. Make an investment in the required equipment yourself, and benefit accordingly.

2. Live without the required equipment, and suffer the consequences. This means that you must accept the fact that you are part of a company that doesn't understand the importance of staying on the cutting edge. But don't complain if this is the choice that you make. Leaders don't complain; they act!

3. In days gone by, the company typically initiated change and the employee automatically followed. If he didn't, the employee was terminated. Today,

due to rapid change, managers don't have time to initiate every required change and still perform all of their other responsibilities. Now, therefore, if the salesperson initiates appropriate technological change, and the company doesn't support him, then he still has the option to "fire" the company and work for a competitor who supports his efforts. It's like the airline traveler who dislikes flying, and people encourage him by saying, "Don't fear, because when it's your time to go, it's your time to go, and not before." This third option is, in effect, the equivalent of the traveler responding, "Fine, but what if it's the pilot's time to go?" Similarly, if the company is destined to sink, you must choose whether to jump ship or go down with it.

It is in this sense—namely, exercising one of the above options—that we say, "YOU are ultimately responsible."

The point is, it is no longer legitimate to take the position toward technology that "I'm going to *wait* and let my boss decide what technology to use," or "I don't have the latest in technology because my boss won't spend the money," or the like.

Technology is now a burgeoning field for you to "seek and find" rather than depend on someone else to deliver to your doorstep. The whole concept of Leadership Selling is that as salespeople we must become more proactive, think more like independent contractors, anticipate what is needed to work best with customers and stay ahead of the competition, and, in short, **lead** rather than follow. It is our experience, and our belief, that most sales managers will appreciate your efforts toward that end.

Your Personal and Professional Development

From this point forth, always understand that the life expectancy of any technology that you purchase is time-limited. You can no longer buy a computer, for example, or a particular software program, take a deep breath of relief, and say to yourself, "I sure am glad to have that expense behind me." Instead, you must budget money and time for continuous upgrades, training and development, and new equipment, just as you must budget for other personal and professional self-development programs.

Most salespeople have long accepted the necessity of investing time and money on a regular basis for such things as product knowledge training, subscribing to various trade publications, and attending industry-related conventions. What we are saying here is that the same rule must hold true for technological advancement. Every salesperson should allocate a certain amount of time and money toward the goal of making sure that he stays technologically current, and to ensure that he is well-informed about what is available today as well as what is on the horizon, and beyond.

Conclusion

"The handwriting is on the wall," as the saying goes, which means that the trend is all too clear. The business world today is changing quickly, faster than anyone could ever have imagined, and it promises only to change more rapidly with each passing day.

The impact of such rapid change on the sales profession is unprecedented. Efficiency has become the name of the game for any salesperson who hopes to thrive. It is time, therefore, for salespeople to face the fact that all inefficient sales behaviors must be eliminated ASAP.

Nothing is more inefficient in a salesperson's life than the strategies used by the vast majority of consumers in their buying processes. Such processes are *profoundly* inefficient because they tend to (1) dupe the seller into giving away his valuable time through presenting information openly and otherwise providing free consulting; (2) put the seller on hold indefinitely while buyers comparison shop, thereby making sellers chase after them; and (3) cause the salesperson to kowtow, beg, and jump through hoops, all of which waste valuable time. In short, buyers have had the luxury of assuming the leadership role and controlling the selling interaction, and sellers have followed the buyer's lead for lack of having a more powerful plan of their own.

The problem, of course, is not that buyers are unscrupulous characters, just as salespeople aren't scoundrels when they are in the buying role and utilize the same processes as consumers. The problem, rather, is that in days past salespeople could still earn a decent living in spite of the humiliation they had to suffer, which in the end made it all worth going through.

It is a different world today, however. Evershortening product life cycles due to rapid technological advancement are causing virtually every product to fast become a commodity. This dynamic presents to the consumer the opportunity to concentrate his attention on price, since products are in such abundant supply. Salespeople subsequently hear from customers on a regular basis that price is *the* primary issue, hence it is understandable that they come to believe that it is true.

But it is **not** true. Customers do **not** buy primarily because of price unless salespeople let them. Price is merely a defense, one among many, that buyers use to protect themselves from feeling the PAIN that is the source of their real buying motives. The successful salesperson today must take the lead by skillfully cutting through the buyer's layers of defense to discover his real PAIN. Once found, the buyer is much more willing to purchase your solution as the way to get out of feeling his PAIN, causing price to become a much lesser issue.

The bottom line is that salespeople must be highly skilled at leading the sales interaction as opposed to continuing to follow the lead of the buyer, which will invariably take the seller straightaway to the price issue. The way to accomplish this is to gain mastery of Leadership Selling, which is designed specifically to help sellers lead through the customer's deceptive maze. This entails not only learning the actual techniques of Leadership Selling, but also developing one's own leadership qualities in order to truly master the system.

The bad news is that until one does so, customers will continue to play the part of the puppeteer to the unsuspecting salesperson, price will become more and more the issue, and inefficiency—and therefore, decreasing sales—will reign. The good news is that when a salesperson truly learns to implement the techniques of Leadership Selling, *he* leads, *he* is in control, *he* becomes more efficient, *he* sells more, and *he* makes more money, as does the company for which he works. Armed with the most advanced selling system in existence today, one that is designed to succeed in *current* as well as in future economic conditions, *you **can** still make the sale*, even *When the Other Guy's Price Is Lower!*

About the Authors

James M. Bleech

Jim is Chairman of the Board of the Leadership Development Center. He is a former CPA and is presently a Certified Professional Consultant to Management. In his 25 years of private industry experience, he has held several executive positions including Chief Operating Officer of a large multi-national construction firm and CEO of a high-profile business in the service sector. Since 1989, Jim has been consulting with leaders in numerous companies ranging from the small entrepreneur to the Fortune 500 senior executive. He is a highly sought-after public speaker and seminar leader. His expertise has been primarily in the areas of sales and marketing growth, and personal leadership skill development for CEOs.

Dr. David G. Mutchler

David is the President and CEO of the Leadership Development Center, a firm that provides leadership services to a wide range of businesses. As a Certified Consultant to Management and a member of the National Bureau of Professional Management Consultants, he is a widely-respected speaker and trainer. After beginning his career as a secondary-school and college instructor, for the past several years David has worked as a sales trainer and business consultant both nationally and internationally. He received a doctorate in psychology and holds graduate degrees in philosophy and social work. His expertise has been primarily in the areas of sales communication, and personal and organizational leadership development.

Let's Get Results, Not Excuses!

A No-Nonsense Approach to Increasing Productivity, Performance and Profit

272 pages/copyright 1995/written for managers and company leaders/a leader's guide to effecting change in corporate America/$14.95

In straightforward, step-by-step language, *Let's Get Results, Not Excuses!* is an amazingly simple but powerful approach to solving corporate problems. As you rid your company of the disease of excuse-making, many other age-old corporate "time-wasters"—such as procrastination, pessimism, projection of blame, denial of responsibility, entitlement, and reactive thinking—also disappear.

- Use the system to **motivate employees** to take responsibility

- Learn how to use a **proven, highly effective formula** by which everyone wins

- Achieve **higher profits** for your company

- Gain the **competitive edge**

- Enhance **teamwork, communication, pride in craftsmanship** and more

Mastering Warp-Speed Change

An Anthology of Great Speakers

James M. Bleech and Dr. David G. Mutchler, in cooperation with several other renowned speakers, have contributed a major chapter in this anthology that bears the same name as the book. The major points of *Mastering Warp-Speed Change* include:

- In years past, companies focused their efforts to become more profitable almost exclusively on increasing the "monies in"—that is, on improving sales.

- Increasingly rapid change that is occurring in the business world today has made it more and more difficult for companies to differentiate themselves and sustain the competitive advantage through monies-in strategies, since products and services can now be so quickly cloned.

- In recent years, therefore, efforts to improve profitability have moved toward decreasing the "monies out" through the likes of corporate reengineering, downsizing, and line-item reductions. The problem is that once all the fat is cut away, there can be no further gain from carving into the "skin and bones" of an already-lean organization.

- The secret to long-term profitability today is to eliminate inefficiency in the workplace—that is, to get rid of the timewasters. The difficulty is that companies haven't always known where to look to find employee inefficiency, nor how to eliminate it if they do find it. *Mastering Warp-Speed Change* emphasizes the critical difference between "managing" one's employees and "leading" them as the key to eliminating inefficiency and increasing profit.